IN THE
MIND'S EYE

Also by Arnold Lazarus
Behavior Therapy Techniques (with Joseph Wolpe)
Behavior Therapy and Beyond
Clinical Behavior Therapy (editor)
Advances in Behavior Therapy (co-editor
     with Richard Rubin, Herbert Fensterheim,
     and Cyril Franks)
I Can If I Want To (with Allen Fay)
Multimodal Behavior Therapy

Arnold Lazarus, Ph.D.

IN THE MIND'S EYE

The Power of Imagery for Personal Enrichment

Rawson Associates Publishers, Inc.
New York

Library of Congress Cataloging in Publication Data
Lazarus, Arnold A
    In the mind's eye.

    Includes index.
    1. Imagery (Psychology). 2. Behavior modification.
I. Title.
BF367.L35   1978   153.8'52   77-88150
ISBN 0-89256-040-1

Published simultaneously in Canada by McClelland and Stewart,
Ltd.
Manufactured in the United States of America
by The Book Press, Brattleboro, Vermont
Designed by *Evelyn O'Connor*
First Edition

CONTENTS

Part I
The Power of Imagery   **1**

1. Imagery Therapy: What It Can Do for You   3
   The Airplane Phobic Executive Woman   5
   The Imagery Vividness Scale   9
   The Use of Associated Imagery   12
2. Imagery—The Key to Many Puzzles   20
   The Step-Up Technique   21
   *Another Example of the Step-Up
      Technique*   23
   The Idealized Self-Image   27
   The Missing Link   30
   Bridging the Gap   32
3. Increasing Your Powers of Imagery   37
   Images and Fear   39
   Where Are Images Stored?   41
   Brain Synchrony Exercises   44

Part II
Using Imagery to Build Confidence and Skill 51

4. Goal Rehearsal to Build Confidence and Skill   53
   *Exaggerated Role-Taking (for Overcoming
      Tension or Anxiety)*   54

Imagery on the Job   58
Goal Rehearsal   61
Assertive Behavior   63
*Goal Rehearsal for Enhancing Athletic
     Performance*   66
Stage Fright   71
Sexual Dysfunctions   72
 5. Overcoming Adult Fears and Anxieties with
     Imagery Techniques   75
Systematic Desensitization   77
Self-Desensitization   82
Social Fears   84
*Other Imagery Methods that Overcome
     Fear*   87
 6. Overcoming Children's Fears and Anxieties
     with Imagery Techniques   95
Applying Emotive Imagery   97
*Batman and Robin Overcome a Child's
     School Phobia*   99
*The Preventive Implications of Positive
     Imagery*   103
*The Basic Steps in Applying Emotive
     Imagery with Children*   105
This Is a Case for Superman!   106

*Part III
Using Imagery to Overcome Problems*   *109*

 7. How Imagery Can Help You Break Habits   111
The Doctor's Fetish   117
The Suicidal Senior   120
*Combining Negative Imagery with
     Positive Rewards*   122
Willpower and Imagery   125

8. The Role of Imagery in Overcoming Sadness
   and Despondency   127
       Time Projection or Time Tripping   131
       Broken Love Affairs   137
       Images of Mastery   141
9. Imagery for Overcoming Psychosomatic
   Disorders   146
       A Cure for Stomach Ulcers?   147
       Hypertension   150
       Dermatitis   151
       Ulcerative Colitis   153
       Spastic Colon   155
       *Tension Headaches (and a Dramatic
         Case of Long-Suppressed Rage)*   156
       Insomnia   161
       Idiosyncratic Imagery   162
10. Imagery for Preventing Future Shock   167
       The Grandmother   171
       Emotional "Fire Drills"   173
       Emotional Stock-Taking   177

Part IV
Some Additional Imagery Exercises   *181*

11. Some Additional Imagery Exercises   183
       *Becoming Less Concerned about Receiving
         Disapproval from Others*   184
       Expressing Honest Opinions   186
       *Saying "No" to Unreasonable or Unwanted
         Requests*   187
       Taking Psychological Risks   188
       The Zero Reaction Image   190
       Concluding Comment   192

CONTENTS

Appendix   193
   Alternate Tension-Relaxation   193
   Sensory Relaxation Training   195
Index   197

viii

PART I

The Power of Imagery

CHAPTER 1

Imagery Therapy: What It Can Do for You

I have used many of the methods described in this book for over twenty years, and for a long time I have been saying: "Some day I'm going to write about imagery, a straightforward book showing how to harness the vast power of mental imagery." Through the proper use of mental imagery, one can achieve an immediate sense of self-confidence, develop more energy and stamina, and tap one's own mind for numerous productive purposes.

You undoubtedly have come across many books that refer to hidden powers of the mind, or that offer mysterious keys to success, or secret methods of mental mastery. Many books refer to mystical notions that lie beyond our own control. This book will remove the mysteries and show you how the process of gaining personal fulfillment can be achieved through straightforward procedures. The emphasis is on *how to change.* You will be given step-by-step procedures for using imagery and fantasy to overcome fear and anxiety, depression, anger, feelings of inferiority, and many other negative emotions. In addition, you will learn how imagery can conquer habits you would like to be rid of, such as smoking and overeating, as well as how it can be tapped to enhance the enjoyable aspects of life—deriving more pleasure from people, becoming more creative at work, gaining proficiency at sports, and improving general patterns of communication.

What do we mean by imagery? For our purposes we are referring only to the dictionary meaning: "a mental picture of something not actually present." For example, if I ask you to tell me how many windows there are in your house, you might close your eyes for a few moments and then come up with an answer. *In order to count the number of windows, you will have to see the house in your mind's eye, to construct a mental image or picture.** Similarly, if we hear the name of a person whom we know very well, we will immediately experience an image of that person. You can easily picture your bedroom, and in a moment you can see yourself hundreds or thousands of miles from home. Next you can imagine being at work, reading some papers, and in a flash you can be in a log cabin, or on a sandy beach, or out with friends, and you can continue to slide effortlessly from scene to scene.

Prisoners in solitary confinement have told how, through active imagery, they have kept themselves

---

* This strategy was first mentioned by Dr. Jerome L. Singer of Yale University, one of the foremost scholars on imagery and fantasy.

from breaking down. By using imagination it is possible to reach out to many realities that are physically absent. Some people claim that they are able to play both sides of chess games in their heads. There are definite differences in people's capacities to form clear and vivid images, but as Dr. Joseph Shorr, director of the Institute of Psycho-Imagination Therapy in Los Angeles, points out, everybody has images in their heads, regardless of what kind of reasoning, wishing, thinking, or problem-solving is going on. If you simply relax and close your eyes, you will most probably have mental pictures. Imagination is sometimes called "the eye of the soul."

This book shows you how to use a variety of images to change both personality and behavior. I have compiled a wide range of imagery procedures and have tested many different imagery techniques. In so doing, I discarded many theories and abandoned a large number of methods that did not prove sufficiently helpful. This process of elimination has left me with a series of imagery techniques that possess amazing power.

THE AIRPLANE PHOBIC EXECUTIVE WOMAN

To demonstrate the powers of imagery let me cite a typical case in point. I was consulted by a female business executive who had worked her way to a top managerial position in a male-dominated organization. She was terrified of traveling by air, but her new position required her to make at least four airplane trips a year to various companies. "I went to a hypnotist who could not help because I did not go into a trance. Then I consulted a psychiatrist who said that my problem is deep-seated and might take years to overcome. What would you advise me to do?"

Her fears had started about four years previously after seeing a film about a plane crash. She had avoided airplanes since then, and the prospect of flying in a plane filled her with terror. She was seriously thinking about giving up her new position. "Right now I have two private secretaries, but perhaps I should quit the company and be a secretary myself. At least I won't have to fly in planes."

Friends had tried to help her with reason and logic. They pointed out that life is full of risks and that statistically, she was safer when traveling by air than when driving a car. "I know all this," she said, "but yet the thought of going in a plane is absolutely terrifying." As we discussed her fears more fully, I saw exactly what was happening to her. Simple word-association tests revealed the following completions: Plane = Crash. Pilot = Danger. Jet = Explode. Landing = Fire. Take-off = Crash. Flight-attendant = Killed. (In the word-association test you present a series of relevant words and ask the person to say the very first word that comes into his or her mind.) It was obvious that this woman did not see airplanes as vehicles that go from destination to destination rapidly, smoothly, and efficiently. In her mind's eye, airplanes inevitably crash on take-off or on landing; they explode in mid-air; their engines stall, their wings fall off, and they become flaming death traps.

I asked her to try to imagine herself in an airplane that reached its destination safely and soundly. She could not do this. Inevitably, she pictured something going wrong. Her most benign image was a message from the pilot. "This is your captain speaking. We have lost the power in two engines. Please put on your life vests. They are under the seat. We are going down. Do not panic." If before going on a journey, you looked into a crystal ball and saw yourself involved in a horrendous accident, wouldn't you avoid the situation? This woman carried around such terrifying images about plane crashes that logic alone could not possibly overcome her phobia. She needed to develop different pictures in her head, a series of positive images about the comfort, efficiency, and safety of air travel.

First we discussed low probability catastrophies (LPCs) and I stressed the fact that life surrounds us with thousands of LPCs. She could slip in her bath, crack her skull, and die. Should she therefore avoid bathtubs? For that matter, another LPC was that the ceiling might fall down and kill her, or she could trip and break her neck. It is utterly neurotic to worry about LPCs. We are certainly wise to avoid high probability catastrophies (HPCs) but the dangers of air travel constitute LPCs, so if she continued avoiding this particular LPC she might start adding others to her list. This simple but compelling evaluation enabled her to pin the correct label to her fears. "It is stupid and counter-productive to dwell on LPCs." Could a plane, while taxiing down the runway, blow a tire, crack up, burst into flames, and kill everyone aboard? Sure, but there is probably a greater risk of choking to death on a piece of steak or of being electrocuted while making toast.

The main treatment strategy consisted of taking her on more and more pleasant imaginary airplane rides. While comfortably ensconced in a large armchair in my office, she would picture herself meeting interesting people on board, sampling some tasty first-class airline food, watching an interesting movie, and enjoying the design and interiors of various DC 8s and Boeing 747s. As she progressed with these images, I added some turbulence, a few "air pockets" and the usual "airplane noises" such as the landing gear and wing flaps being lowered.

Approximately two months later, after eight imagery sessions plus homework exercises in positive imagery, she went on her first plane trip—a relatively short hop from New York to Washington, D.C. She had reserved a return trip on the train "just in case," but she decided to fly back instead. "I loved it," she told me. "I was not the least bit afraid. I just felt comfortable and completely safe." And then she joked with me, "But now I am terrified of eating steak, making toast, and of taking a bath."

Today, almost four years after first consulting me about her airplane phobia, this woman has flown thousands of miles here and abroad. She has gained further promotion at work and also manages to be a creative wife and mother. Please note how the use of imagery overcame her phobia without resorting to formal hypnosis or traditional psychiatry. More examples of overcoming phobias with imagery techniques will be given in Chapter 5, and throughout this book, specific imagery exercises will be presented to enrich the quality of life. You will be shown exactly how to use certain images for overcoming fear and sadness, for breaking bad habits, controlling psychosomatic illnesses, improving athletic ability, and even for preventing "future shock" and coping with life's inevitable crises.

As one might expect, there is a wide range of individual differences in people's capacities to form vivid images. Some of us can conjure up perfectly distinct images that are as clear as the actual event. Others possess "very clear" (but not perfect) imagery. The scale below, on which you can rate yourself, extends through "moderately clear," "fairly clear," "vague or unclear," to "indiscernible." In order to derive benefit from the imagery exercises in this book, *you need only form fairly clear images.* Of course, if you can form "moderately clear" or "very clear" images, so much the better.

THE IMAGERY VIVIDNESS SCALE

Let's try a simple test. You will be asked to picture certain images. If your image is "very clear" give it a rating of 4; if "moderately clear" give it a 3; a "fairly clear" image rates a 2; and an "unclear" image rates a 1. If you cannot form an image, or if it is "very unclear" or "indiscernible," give it 0. After reading each item, close your eyes, picture it as clearly as you can, and then record your own rating.

Think about a very close relative or friend:

		Rating
1.	See him/her standing in front of you.	( )
2.	Imagine him/her laughing.	( )
3.	Picture his/her eyes.	( )
4.	Picture a bowl of fruit.	( )
5.	Imagine driving down a dry, dusty road.	( )
6.	See yourself throwing a ball.	( )
7.	Picture your childhood home.	( )
8.	See a white, sandy beach.	( )
9.	Imagine looking into a shop window.	( )
10.	See a blank television screen.	( )
11.	Imagine the sound of a barking dog.	( )
12.	Imagine the sound of an exploding firecracker.	( )
13.	Feel the warmth of a hot shower.	( )
14.	Imagine feeling the texture of rough sandpaper.	( )
15.	Picture yourself lifting a heavy object.	( )

16. Imagine yourself walking up a
    steep stairway.   ( )
17. Imagine the taste of lemon
    juice.   ( )
18. Think of eating ice cream.   ( )
19. Imagine the smell of cooking
    cabbage.   ( )
20. Imagine yourself smelling a
    rose.   ( )

A perfect score of 80 would imply that each of the ratings received a 4 and were seen (or felt, smelled, tasted, or experienced) as *very clear*. Few people will score 80. If your score is 60 or more, it means that you have well-developed powers of imagery. If your total score is less than 30, I doubt if this book will be of much help to you. Perhaps extensive training in imagery might render you more able to form fairly clear images, but you will probably be better off with a different approach. However, if you scored 30 or more points on this test, I would say there is every reason to believe that imagery techniques will be of immense benefit to you.

The present book, in keeping with a current trend toward *self-management,* presents a take-home series of imagery exercises and procedures. Certain imagery techniques require the presence of a therapist who can guide the particular fantasies and protect us from possible sensitizing or upsetting experiences. These kinds of imagery methods are not included here. The majority of imagery techniques do not require a therapist to be present in order to derive full benefit. Although I (a therapist) am present in most of the examples given in this book, please understand that you can readily apply these methods on your own. Most of the people who consult me have applied imagery on their own as homework assignments. The best and most rapid results were obtained by those who did their homework regularly and conscientiously.

So many people feel a sense of powerlessness. The systematic application of imagery exercises can provide an enduring sense of personal power and control. This book, based upon my own clinical findings as well as those of other therapists, will show you exactly how to use your images and fantasies to enhance the quality of your life.

In thinking back over numerous people with whom I have used imagery methods, and in reviewing hundreds of case records, I am impressed by the fact that real and significant gains so frequently accrued as soon as imagery was employed. Throughout this book, many case examples and specific imagery exercises will be described, but at this point it may prove illuminating to outline one of my favorite clinical techniques.

THE USE OF ASSOCIATED IMAGERY

PATIENT: I've still been feeling uptight and depressed. I don't know what's gotten into me. I'm not doing my work properly and everything's going to pieces.

THERAPIST: Well, we have certainly looked into all sorts of reasons behind your anxiety and tension and we have tried various methods to help you conquer your fears. Often the use of imagery helps where all other things have failed.

PATIENT: What do you mean?

THERAPIST: Let me show you. Just sit back comfortably, try to relax, let your body get loose and heavy, take in a few deep breaths, let the air in and out. . . . Close your eyes, and try to imagine yourself somewhere, doing something that makes you feel very calm and peaceful. Take your time. (Pause of about one minute.) What's happening? Your breathing seems to be slow and even, and you appear to be relaxed. What were you picturing?

PATIENT: (Opens eyes.) For some reason I saw myself on a farm watching some people milking the cows, and a lot of other pictures went flashing through my mind.

THERAPIST: Such as?

PATIENT: I can't remember most of them, but a lot of things that I did as a kid came back to me. I used to love working on the farm.

THERAPIST: Let's try a simple experiment. Can you get into your uptight, anxious, and depressed feelings? Try to make yourself feel really tense.

PATIENT: That's very easy for me! (After a few moments) I can feel it now. I've even got butterflies in my stomach.

13

THERAPIST: How did you bring on the negative feelings? What ideas, thoughts, images, or pictures did you focus on?

PATIENT: I don't know.

THERAPIST: Come on. You must have thought about something. Did you think about milking cows?

PATIENT: No. (Pause) I guess I just thought about being anxious, about falling apart. I wasn't thinking about anything specific.

THERAPIST: Get back into those anxious feelings. Let them grow really strong. (Pause) Now as you are feeling really uptight, flash back to any scene in your past. Quick. What do you see?

PATIENT: Do you know what came to mind? For some reason I thought about the pony my father bought me when I was ten. Now what can you make of that?

THERAPIST: Picture the pony as clearly as you can. Close your eyes and visualize the pony.

PATIENT: (Becoming visibly upset) The pony broke his leg and they had to destroy him.

THERAPIST: Are you talking about an image?

PATIENT: (Weeping) No. It really happened. My oldest brother was riding him and the pony stepped into a pothole. I'm feeling terribly anxious right now.

THERAPIST: We might be on to something. Try to picture your brother riding the pony. What images do you see?

PATIENT: I can't picture that. I just draw a blank.

THERAPIST: Just let yourself relax. Sit back in the chair. Let go of the tension. Breathe in and out, and each time you breathe out, feel the tension leaving your body. (30 second pause) Now try to picture your brother riding the pony.

PATIENT: (Long pause)

THERAPIST: What images do you see?

PATIENT: It's most peculiar. I can't get a clear picture of my brother. I imagine him on the pony and then I suddenly see myself riding it. We sort of alternate.

THERAPIST: Do you ever merge?

PATIENT: How do you mean?

THERAPIST: In the image, are you unable to separate yourself from your brother?

PATIENT: I don't know. It's not very clear.

THERAPIST: Let's try it again. Take your time, relax, settle down, breathe easy, and then try to picture your brother riding the pony.

PATIENT: (After about 30 seconds, opens eyes) Yes, we do merge. I fade in and out and so does my brother. It's hard to tell if it's me or my brother on the pony.

THERAPIST: Are we talking about the brother that died several years ago?

PATIENT: Yes. My oldest brother.

THERAPIST: Let's see. He was eight years older than you?

PATIENT: That's right. My other brothers are six years and four years younger than me. I don't see where this is leading, and I don't mean to change the subject, but I should mention that I'm feeling quite sick.

THERAPIST: Where are you feeling ill?

15

PATIENT: My head hurts, I feel dizzy, and my chest feels tight.

THERAPIST: Yes, you look and sound upset and anxious. But I have more than a hunch about what is going on with you. Just bear with me. How old was your brother when he died?

PATIENT: Fifty-two when he had a heart attack.

THERAPIST: And you are now fifty-one years old.

PATIENT: So?

THERAPIST: Why do you think you merged with your brother in the imagery exercise?

PATIENT: What are you driving at?

THERAPIST: Well, we've been totally unable to explain how come you suddenly started feeling anxious and depressed a few months ago. There seems to be no logical reason for it. Everything seems to be going well with you, but over the past months you have been feeling more and more upset, uptight, miserable . . .

PATIENT: And you think it's tied in with my brother?

THERAPIST: Well, do you have any sort of gut reaction to this idea? Perhaps in many ways you over-identified with your older brother. I think that you have emulated him in many ways. Anyway, he died at fifty-two from a heart attack, and I think that a part of you believes that your destiny is tied up with his and that you will go the same way when you reach fifty-two.

PATIENT: That's why I'm so anxious?

THERAPIST: Does it sound far-fetched?

PATIENT: I don't know. I mean I can't say yes or no.

THERAPIST: Let's try out some more imagery. Try to

close your eyes and relax as best as you can. (Pause of about 40 seconds) Now picture your brother standing in front of you. See him as clearly, as vividly as possible.

PATIENT: (After about 30 seconds) I can't! I think you're right. I keep seeing him change into me or me into him. Say, if this is the problem, how can I cope with it?

THERAPIST: Let's start with simple exercises. Relax again, close your eyes, and keep saying inwardly to yourself over and over again: "I am not my brother; I am myself." Do this now for a few minutes.

PATIENT: (After about a minute) You know, it does make me feel much less anxious. . . .

Commentary: As further facts emerged, the initial hypothesis had to be extended, but the imagery methods were the thin end of a wedge that pried open a basic reason for the patient's persistent anxiety. The use of imagery can often bypass verbal roadblocks and get to the root of the matter. Many people tend to over-intellectualize and they confuse everybody and themselves with verbiage. Imagery methods can permit a therapist to side-step these barriers.

Associated imagery can be most useful in tracking down the reasons behind everyday upsets. Obviously, when dealing with high degrees of anxiety, depression, and other emotional disturbances, a trained professional is essential. However, if you feel tense, or nervous, or otherwise upset, and you are unable to pinpoint why you are feeling bad, here is how you might use associated imagery.

1. Try to relax as much as possible (See the appendix for relaxation exercises.)

2. Then return to the negative feelings and try to increase them. Thus, if you are feeling nervous, make yourself feel even more nervous; if angry, let your anger grow more intense.

3. Immediately focus on any image that comes to mind. Whatever that image happens to be, see it as vividly as possible. (Most people prefer doing imagery exercises with their eyes closed, but this is not essential.)

4. As you keep focusing on the image, others may take its place. If so, try to see each one as clearly as possible.

5. If different images do not come to mind, zero in on the original image as if using a zoom lens. Get really close up to it. This will assist you in associating different parts of the same image more meaningfully, or it will evoke other images for you to track.

6. As you follow each image, you may return to some of them, or to parts of these images. Just keep on seeing the images as clearly as you can.

This simple exercise often permits interesting insights and self-revelations to come to mind. Brilliant scholars such as William James, who wrote extensively about the stream of consciousness, and Sigmund Freud, who pioneered the use of free association, were well aware of the value of dipping into and tracking down elements of on-going thought processes. The technique of associated imagery is tied in with many theories that explain the virtues of sampling the free-flowing and kaleidoscopic pictures and events that pass through the mind's eye.

The next chapter outlines a more highly structured technique for achieving the same result. I call it the Step-Up technique.

CHAPTER 2

Imagery—The Key to Many Puzzles

An understanding of the role that imagery plays in our daily lives provides a clue to unraveling otherwise insoluble puzzles. For example, I was recently consulted by a young woman who complained that she felt unhappy, confused, and anxious. She explained that she developed these symptoms immediately after receiving a raise at work. "I was told that I would be moved up to another department, that I would be in charge of buying in that department, and that I would take home more than twenty-five dollars a week in extra pay. . . . Although I was very pleased about the extra money and I also liked the sound of my new responsibilities, I immediately became panicky . . . I'm confused because there is no reason for me to feel less than one hundred percent happy about my promotion." She was to assume her new duties within three weeks and wondered what to do about her situation.

Practicing therapists encounter puzzles such as this over and over again. What was really disturbing this woman? Many ideas came to mind. Was she afraid that she wouldn't cope with the added responsibility? Did she feel unworthy of the raise? Would this new work situation prevent her from having a family? Would her husband harbor some resentments? Would her friends become jealous? We discussed each of these possibilities and checked out several other hunches, but we continued to draw a blank. I then used a simple imagery technique.

THE STEP-UP TECHNIQUE

I asked her to sit back comfortably, to close her eyes, to let go of her tension, to feel relaxed and calm. After a few minutes of relaxation, I asked her to visualize herself at work. "See yourself at work in the new department. Take your time and picture yourself working there. What do you see?"

She described a series of activities—dealing with customers, advising salespeople, interviewing sales representatives, computing sales figures, ordering merchandise. None of these scenes provoked any feelings of discomfort in her, and the puzzle remained unsolved. Then I stepped up the image.

"See yourself being promoted even higher up in the firm. You are now a vice president of the company." After a few moments she opened her eyes and sat upright in the chair. "Now I'm beginning to see what's bothering me."

A significant fact emerged. As she toyed with the image of being vice president, she realized that the idea was not far-fetched, that she very well might attain a senior position within two years. She allowed this idea to sink in for several minutes. "That's where the trouble comes in," she explained. "I have all kinds of vague schemes over the next five years, and the image of being seduced by my present job makes me feel very scared. If I have it too good I might end up staying there and later on regret it." After further discussion she added, "I want to do well in my job, but I'm afraid to do too well in case I am tempted to end up doing something boring for the sake of money and prestige." Now we were able to discuss her uncertainties and her temptations and arrive at a logical solution.

This example shows the way in which imagery was used for diagnostic purposes. A straightforward image can often solve puzzling situations. If you cannot account for some of your own actions and feelings, try picturing yourself in the situations that create these reactions. If no answers emerge, remember the Step-Up technique. That is, take the image a few steps further than the real situation. You may begin to discover something you had not realized about yourself.

One of the main reasons the Step-Up technique proves so helpful is that it pushes through a barrier of natural resistance. It is human nature to back away from unpleasant thoughts, images, feelings, and events. When situations are distasteful or disagreeable, the tendency is to avoid them. But when we avoid thinking about and working through negative emotions we seldom conquer them. By stepping up the potential consequences, we not only face reality, but we also transcend the situation and can view it more dispassionately. In this way we can gain clearer insight and also devise methods of dealing with adversity. The following example will illustrate these points quite clearly.

ANOTHER EXAMPLE OF THE STEP-UP TECHNIQUE

As indicated in the previous case, the Step-Up technique can shed diagnostic light on one's problems, but as the next case will illustrate, it can also be used to dispel anxiety.

A student complained that he was extremely anxious about his final examinations. "I feel so uptight," he complained, "that I can't concentrate. I'm sure I'm going to fail." I asked him what would happen if he failed. He cited a host of familiar themes—letting down his parents, looking foolish to his peers, feeling bad about himself. When I tried to emphasize that his failure, although disappointing and inconvenient, would not be terrible or catastrophic, he insisted that the consequences of failing his finals would be awful and dreadful.

Since we got nowhere with rational disputation, I decided to employ the Step-Up technique. First, I asked him to close his eyes and let his muscles go loose. He relaxed as well as he could, and I had him picture himself failing his final examinations. I then stepped up the consequences. Instead of merely disappointing his parents, he was to visualize them completely disowning him; likewise, he was to picture his peers abandoning him, the school refusing to re-admit him, so that he became a veritable pariah. "What will you do now?" I asked him. After a few moments of thought, he said that he would move to another country and start all over again. Thus, even in the face of impossibly harsh rejection he could see that life goes on. We ended the session on that note.

He telephoned me a few days later to report that his studies were proceeding well because his extreme anxiety had abated. I was very pleased, but not surprised. The Step-Up technique often enables us to see matters in their true perspective. Now he was aware that if he failed an examination, his life would not come to an end. Thus he was able to do his best, and to hope for the best.

The Step-Up technique has many applications. We often have to face situations about which we are less than pleased, or over which we are most concerned. "I am being audited by the IRS!" "I'm applying to medical school." "I'm going for an interview." "I'm supposed to give a public talk next week." In all these instances, if the people are unduly anxious, the Step-Up technique can prove most helpful. One simply pictures the worst thing that can happen, and then one vividly imagines oneself coping with the situation—surviving even the most negative outcome.* By contrast, when the real situation rolls round, it is most unlikely to be a quarter as

---

* Some people are so deeply negative that they simply find themselves totally incapable of imagining themselves coping positively. These people usually require much more intensive imagery training than this book provides.

bad as the horrors that one has deliberately called into fantasy.

I used the Step-Up technique with a woman who had been through a traumatic marriage and an even uglier divorce and who was extremely afraid of any further male-female involvements. Men were asking her out on dates but she turned them all down. She was lonely, frightened, lacked confidence, and felt inferior. Her ex-husband had led her to believe that she was sexless and unattractive. In truth, most people found her very attractive and vivacious. Attempts to reassure her proved futile. I asked her why so many men wanted her to go out with them if she was so unattractive. She said that it was probably out of pity. I then asked her what would happen if she accepted one of these invitations. "Oh! I don't know," she replied, "they'd probably regret it and I would be taken home very early." That's when I decided to use the Step-Up technique.

I asked her to get comfortable, to relax, to close her eyes, and to picture some scenes that I would describe. She had accepted an invitation from a man whom she found most attractive and charming. He picked her up and they drove to an excellent restaurant for dinner. He was charming, interesting, and very pleasant throughout the evening, but as he drove her home, he turned to her and said: "I feel compelled to tell you that you are the worst bore that I have ever dated. You are about as interesting as an old dishrag, and now that I have looked at you closely, I realize how plain and insipid you really are. You have no redeeming features, and believe me when I tell you that I have looked hard to find some. Everything about you is wrong—I dislike the way you walk, the way you talk, and even the way in which you eat, how you sit, how you move, and how you breathe. Your choice of clothes is tasteless and it is obvious that your body is as sexy as yesterday's garbage. Your husband must be a saint for having put up with you for as long as he did."

She started smiling when I said "yesterday's garbage," and she burst into laughter when I added the sentence about her husband. She opened her eyes and said, "Nobody would ever say all those things!" I agreed with her but added, "Perhaps they would *think* those things to themselves." We then repeated the sequence, only this time we had her being driven home in silence while her date was thinking to himself how much he regretted wasting money on her, how unintelligent and utterly tedious and downright ugly she turned out to be. I had her picture herself receiving criticism and put downs for everything from her fingernails to her values and opinions.

When I saw her ten days later she informed me that she had been out six times that week with two different men. She explained: "When they asked me out I figured I had nothing to lose. I mean after the things you had put me through, everything else would be an anticlimax. No matter what any of them would say to me I would know that I had heard worse things, much worse things." Thus, the Step-Up technique broke up yet another emotional log jam.

In addition to the Step-Up technique, there are

26

dozens of simple, straightforward, but eminently effective imagery techniques. In this book I have selected those specific imagery methods that have proved particularly useful and helpful. In the final analysis, our images color and produce our emotions. Sad, angry, and anxious feelings are caused by self-destructive images. Our images also serve as self-fulfilling prophecies—if we picture ourselves failing to cope with adversity, we are likely to end up with emotional difficulties. Conversely, and this is one of the main points of the book, if we systematically and repeatedly picture ourselves being successful and achieving our goals, there is generally a predictable transfer from imagery to reality.

THE IDEALIZED SELF-IMAGE

The use of success-oriented images is perhaps best exemplified by a technique known as ISI (Idealized Self-Image). Developed by Dr. Dorothy Susskind of Hunter College in the City University of New York, this imagery method is designed to help people who suffer from a lack of self-confidence, together with poor self-esteem. The ISI involves the following steps:

1. Relax as comfortably as you can (see appendix) and then close your eyes and picture yourself possessing various qualities and skills that you would like to have. Do not select an ISI that is beyond your capacity, but try to see yourself attaining

various attributes that can be achieved in a relatively short time period. Try to be as specific as possible. For example, do not say, "I want to be successful," because this is too vague. Instead, see yourself developing poise, intellectual curiosity, a better way of relating to people, and so forth.

2. In your mind's eye, carefully contrast and compare your ISI with your actual self-image. This will enable you to set specific goals so that you can participate actively toward achieving the new behaviors you desire.

3. Part of self-confidence building is recalling something that you did quite well. Dwell on that incident and recapture whatever feelings of achievement and accomplishment you can muster.

4. Transfer and extend this feeling of achievement and success to your ongoing activities. Apply it to anything you are doing at present and plan to do in the immediate future.

5. Keep on bringing your ISI into clear focus. Whatever you are doing—talking to friends, walking down the street, attending a business meeting—identify with your ISI. When you discover a discrepancy between your real self and your ideal self, ask yourself exactly what you are doing that is incorrect. Picture yourself changing your tactics. Begin to act and feel more like your ISI.

A brief case outline might help to clarify the way in which the ISI can be applied. A 24-year-old woman was overweight, anxious about speaking in class (she was taking a course in English literature), and she was inclined to feel awkward in many social situations. Her ISI differed from her actual self-image in these three respects—she saw herself as slim rather than fat, she imagined herself asking questions and making comments in class, and she pictured herself being calm and relaxed at social gatherings. She kept this ISI in her mind whenever she had a moment to think about it. Day after day she vividly saw herself being slim and non-anxious. Slowly, her positive image started transferring to the actual situations. When tempted to eat fattening foods she would think of her ISI and adhere to her diet. In class, she pictured her ISI and took the risk of speaking up on a few occasions. This led her to feel much more at ease in class, and she took similar risks socially. "Usually, I would refrain from asking strangers any questions, but in my ISI I saw myself acting very differently, so I decided to act more like the 'new me' and I'm glad I did."

As Dr. Susskind points out, when we focus upon our mistakes, dwell on our inadequacies, and think about our rejections, we end up expecting to fail, and this negative view becomes a "self-fulfilling prophecy." The ISI technique provides essential ingredients for the development of a more constructive life style.

The ISI is only one of numerous techniques that will be described in this book to alter self-defeating life patterns into constructive outlets, positive identity, and enhanced self-esteem.

THE MISSING LINK

Everyone knows that no two people are alike. Different individuals respond to the same situation in different ways. Take the case of two young athletes who were both badly injured in an accident and would never be able to enter athletic competitions again. One young man was extremely depressed and suicidal. He felt that life had lost all meaning for him. The other man, equally disabled, was calm, confident, and even optimistic. What was the essential ingredient that led to such opposite reactions? *Different imagery.*

The first athlete focused on what he had lost, on what he did not possess, on what he could no longer achieve, on what he might have been, on the misfortune that had befallen him. The other young man concentrated instead upon his positive attributes, not on what he had lost, but on what he still possessed. When interviewed he said that he was competitive by training and inclination, that he would switch from athletics to bridge, chess, and other sedentary games, and that he would probably end up winning championships and tournaments. Thus, one person sees himself all washed up and ready for the morgue, the other pictures himself learning new skills and enjoying the thrill of new-found success. Different images produce different behaviors, different feelings and sensations, different thoughts and perceptions, and different problem-solving strategies.

Many people will ask how and why these two

athletes developed such antithetical styles of responding to their problems. The answer to this question is complex and involves an understanding of the interplay of temperament, formative childhood encounters, and the acquisition of problem-solving skills in general. However, the main question for our purposes is whether or not people such as the unhappy and suicidal athlete can be taught to employ positive imagery in place of their destructive and nihilistic precepts. Fortunately, the answer in most cases is *yes*. And that's what this book is all about.

Often, personal misunderstandings and emotional clashes can be prevented by articulating the missing link—the unspoken image. For example, husband and wife decide to spend a weekend in a motel "just for fun." The husband's image is that they will spend nearly all of the time sleeping, making love, having room service, and perhaps watching one or two TV programs. The wife, on the other hand, has a series of images involving tennis, an indoor pool, dancing, and socializing with other couples. This pair had better align their divergent images before setting out on their venture or their anticipated "fun" might turn to gloom. The classic example is depicted in a cartoon of newlyweds driving away in their wedding car. The husband pictures himself relaxing in comfort while his wife serves him breakfast in bed. The wife has the same image, except that she sees her husband doing the serving.

And talking about "missing links," a serious consideration facing many managerial and executive women today is the absence of a meaningful link—

they do not possess a clear image of their respective roles and interpersonal functions. There are too few role models for corporate women to emulate, and they often battle to find a productive and acceptable way of relating to fellow workers, be they men or women. Many top-level women find it difficult to be assertive without appearing aggressive, and to remain feminine without seeming coy or maternal. Here the use of exaggerated role-taking and goal rehearsal (see Chapter 4) can be extremely helpful. In this connection, many women need to learn that the business game must be played a certain way. Women who resort to traditional feminine wiles in business dealings will probably lose out in the end. The successful female executive avoids "feminine manipulation"—she does not cry, or sulk, or pout, or resort to moody tactics. Whether one is wearing trousers or a skirt, successful business negotiations depend upon a series of self-images in which one sees oneself possessing poise, humor, assertion, tact, and discretion. Here again, goal rehearsal (see Chapter 4) can prove most valuable.

BRIDGING THE GAP

As one delves into the vast richness of inner images and subjective meanings the limitations of stimulus-response psychology become apparent. Referred to as S-R theory, adherents of this approach believe that you can understand, predict, and control responses (Rs) if you know the antecedent stimuli (Ss). But the diverse ways in which different people react to the same stimuli, and the different ways in which the same individual will react to similar stimuli at different times, indicates that something else is going on between the stimulus (S) and the response (R). *Many therapists now believe that an image, or a series of images, bridges the stimulus and the response.*

Here is a typical example. A group of people are sitting around a fireplace having a pleasant social evening. Suddenly a friendly puppy bounds into the room and starts licking some of the guests. One of them immediately grows pale, starts trembling, and shouts, "Keep that dog away from me!" In S-R terms, the entry of the puppy would be the *stimulus,* and the guest's outburst is the *response.*

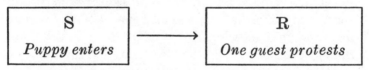

The response makes no logical sense in the face of the stimulus. If a ferocious dog had entered the room and had started growling at the people, the person's cry of "Keep that dog away from me!" would make immediate sense.

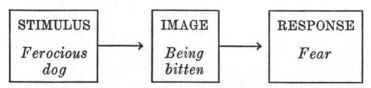

Observe that we have interposed an *image* between the stimulus and the response. It is not the ferocious dog per se that engenders the fear. Let us suppose that a dog twice as fierce and savage was locked in a steel cage. Would the stimulus "ferocious dog" still elicit the same fear response? Of course not—unless someone had the image of the dog escaping from the cage!

The previous examples all point to a highly significant fact. The missing link between various stimuli and responses turns out to be some form of *imagery*. In the case of the person who reacted so violently to the friendly puppy, an exploration of his imagery revealed the reasons behind the behavior. He had the image of the puppy snapping at him, biting his ankle, inflicting pain, tearing his trousers and, above all, he pictured himself developing a severely infected wound that would require medical attention. (Years before, he had been bitten by a small dog and had developed a painful infection.) Thus, many seemingly inexplicable stimulus-response connections make sense as soon as we understand the intervening imagery.

STIMULUS ⟶ IMAGERY ⟶ RESPONSE

Every event will be transposed into images and thoughts. Everything that we experience is filed in the mind and exerts an influence on our actions. Our beliefs govern all our responses. Thousands of years ago, a Greek philospoher, Epictetus, wrote the following:

What disturbs men's minds is not events but their judgments on events. . . . And so when we are hindered, or disturbed, or distressed, let us never lay the blame on others, but on ourselves, that is, on our own judgments. To accuse others for one's own misfortunes is a sign of want of education; to accuse oneself shows that one's education has begun; to accuse neither oneself nor others shows that one's education is complete.

It is astonishing to realize that these brilliant observations were made in the first century A.D. They form the cornerstone of rational thinking in psychotherapy, and have been refined and amplified by Dr. Albert Ellis, the Executive Director of the Institute for Advanced Study in Rational Psychotherapy, New York City.

The "judgments" to which Epictetus referred have been shown by Dr. Albert Ellis to consist of "self-talk" (i.e., statements, sentences, and reflections about current happenings). Dr. Aaron T. Beck, Professor of Psychiatry at the School of Medicine of the University of Pennsylvania, stresses that "rapid thoughts or images occur between an activating event and the emotional response." Indeed, many authorities now agree that in accounting for the vagaries of human behavior, there is no need to speculate about unconscious complexes, hidden forces, demons, or even conditioned reflexes. Words, ideas, values, attitudes, and beliefs are all replete with imagery. *Find* the images and you will understand the behavior. Furthermore, find the images and, if you so desire, you will probably be able to *change* the feelings and the behavior.

Before turning to specific imagery exercises and case studies which show how imagery can be used to overcome various emotional problems, some readers might like to have a more detailed explanation of imagery processes. The next chapter touches on several theoretical and background factors.

CHAPTER 3

Increasing Your
Powers of Imagery

We hear much about the "unconscious mind" and about occult forces that lie beneath our levels of awareness. According to certain authorities, a whirlpool of subconscious activity extends into the dark reaches of the mind and governs many of our feelings and behaviors. Some people believe that we are the victims of deeply repressed impulses and mysterious energies that ultimately control our actions. Theorists who are deeply committed to these views seldom see things for what they are. They regard everything about personal interaction as symbolic of something more fundamental. Pride is inverted hate; joy is displaced grief. They see creativity as sexual sublimation, and ambition as overcompensated inferiority!

Why have so many theorists resorted to these complex and mystifying interpretations of human behavior? Part of the answer lies in the fact that human beings are by nature problem solvers, and we generally find fascination in complex rather than simple phenomena. How can something as intricate as the human mind be orchestrated by straightforward processes? And yet modern research, without disputing the delicate, subtle, and often inexplicable convolutions of mind and brain, has nevertheless revealed many uncomplicated facts about human psychology.

Many people do not realize that we all think on verbal and nonverbal levels. When dwelling on important concerns, a wide range of pictures and images inevitably accompanies, and feeds into, our emotions.

Will you test this out for yourself?

Think of anything that makes you feel especially *glad*. Take your time, put down this book for a few moments and reflect about those situations or events that produce happy, pleasant, good, and wholesome feelings in you.

After dwelling on those pleasant associations, turn your thoughts to matters and events that make you feel *sad*. What leads you to feel dejected, disheartened, gloomy, downcast, in the dumps?

Stop. Put down this book. Think . . .

And now, try to think about anything that makes you *mad*. What sorts of things lead you to feel angry, hostile, or even enraged?

Stop. Put down this book. Think . . .

Finally, focus on things that make you feel *scared*. What are the stimuli that make you uptight, afraid, anxious, apprehensive, or frightened?

Stop. Put down this book. Think . . .

* * *

Now let's examine what was going through your head during this exercise. Were you thinking solely in words or sentences? Did any pictures or images flash through your mind, however hazy or fleeting they were? The vast majority of people will have no difficulty in realizing that when experiencing any significant feelings or sensations, a series of mental pictures or images soon comes into being.

And yet the significance and the power of mental imagery has been underplayed by a great many psychologists and psychiatrists. They seldom recognize that certain images can *cause* many emotional problems. But perhaps more important, many professionals remain unaware that the deliberate and concerted use of specific images often proves to be the key that unlocks and opens the way to solve hitherto puzzling problems. Imagery opens up one of the most powerful areas of personality for overcoming innumerable daily stresses. It also provides an effective tool for developing a more rational approach to many different problems.

IMAGES AND FEAR

A 35-year-old real estate salesman lived and worked in New Jersey. He enjoyed his work, earned a good living, had a happy family life, but for the past ten years had refused to cross bridges or drive through tunnels. As far back as he could recall, he had been afraid of bridges and tunnels, a fear that he ascribed to some horror stories he had heard as a very young child. His fears readily came to the fore after a distant acquaintance was killed when his car went over the side of a bridge; the accident made headline news.

The realtor now wished to travel from New Jersey into New York City because some lucrative business opportunities had arisen. To cross the Hudson River from New Jersey into New York, one must enter a tunnel or cross a bridge. On separate occasions he traveled by bus and by train and reported that "both times I thought I was dying from a heart attack. . . . I became so anxious that I could hardly breathe." The thought of driving his own car was completely out of the question. When asked why he was so terrified of bridges and tunnels he said there was no logical reason. He was completely puzzled. "I realize that the odds against something happening are more than a million to one." (Dr. Aaron Beck's work has shown that a person's perceived chances of catastrophe tend to increase drastically as one approaches the phobic object.)

I asked him to imagine being on a bridge or in a tunnel, to picture it vividly and realistically. At first, he drew a blank and seemed to be resisting the idea, but gradually, as he allowed the image to grow clear, he reported that as he approached a tunnel or a bridge in imagination, he experienced, with increasing clarity, the image of the bridge collapsing or the tunnel caving in. "I imagine that I can hear a strange rumble, then it grows a little louder. Suddenly there is a dreadful lurching, a terrible shudder. Then my imagination plays more tricks on me. . . . When the bridge or the tunnel collapses, there is virtually no sound. Although steel and concrete and iron are being crushed, it is all terrifyingly quiet.'' Next, he automatically pictured a flood of images involving drowning and suffocation. These images clearly showed the mechanisms behind his phobia. Anyone with such terrifying images would be likely to avoid situations that evoked them. (Chapter 5 describes exactly how one goes about changing the aversive images that can create an almost endless variety of specific fears.)

WHERE ARE IMAGES STORED?

The brain has often been likened to an extremely intricate and dynamic computer. It may also be said to have several "cameras" that constantly photograph and record a myriad of pictures—black and white, color, slides, as well as motion pictures replete with sound tracks. These pictures or *mental images* are stored in various "albums" and "libraries" in our minds and are often called forth and used to our advantage or disadvantage. Some of the most dramatic evidence about the way in which the brain stores memory traces, as well as visual and auditory images, comes from the field of brain surgery. The brain itself, or the cerebral cortex, can be cut without any reports of pain. A local anesthetic is used to prevent pain while the head is being penetrated prior to the brain surgery, but during many brain operations the patient remains awake. While operating upon the brain of several patients to alleviate certain forms of epileptic seizures, Dr.

41

Wilder Penfield, a neurosurgeon from Montreal, and his associates stimulated various parts of the brain with weak electrical currents and aroused *imagery of past experiences*. These images were visual or auditory, or both, and the same image could be evoked repeatedly by successively stimulating the same spot. People who were stimulated in some regions of the brain reported hearing music or seeing flashing lights; other points in the associative cortex were then stimulated and the patients experienced a variety of different images.

When one point was electrically stimulated, a patient said that she heard a mother calling her boy. She added that this memory went back many years. Each time that particular point was stimulated, this elicited further reports about the voice calling. Various details were added, such as the fact that this scene was taking place in a lumberyard. When stimulated at different points of the brain, the patient recalled other images such as seeing a circus wagon, watching a play, and several memories of an office where she had once worked as a stenographer.

Thus it would seem that people, places, scenes, events, and innumerable personal happenings are "photographed" or "recorded" and filed away in the convolutions of our cerebral cortex. Weak electrical stimuli applied to our exposed brain can elicit random images, but so can millions of other stimuli. The word "RED!" or the phrase "A hot summer's day," or the statement "Think of elephants!" will evoke various images, if you stop and think about them for a moment. There are obviously thousands of random images and associations, but important or significant images are just as easily evoked. "Think of your parent's faces. See their faces as vividly as possible." If you concentrate on this significant image for a few moments you will probably experience a variety of feelings and emotions, and have a stream of associations. This book will discuss numerous meaningful images, and will show you how to conjure them up and how to put them to work for you.

During the past ten years, new data regarding the separate functions of the right and left hemisphere of the brain have emerged. It is generally recognized that each side of the brain controls the opposite side of the body. However, while the left hemisphere controls the right side of the body, it is also responsible for logical thinking, speech and verbal activity, reading, writing, sequential ordering, and analytic processing. The left brain is predominantly involved with rational and orderly thinking; it processes information one bit after another.

The right hemisphere of the brain is quite the opposite. While controlling the left side of the body, one of its most obvious faculties is the comprehension of visual images. The right side of the brain is not logical or sequential, but operates in a more holistic, simultaneous, relational way. It is intuitive, emotional, and is involved in spatial relations. Whereas artists, certain intuitive philosophers, sculptors, and musicians may have well-developed right-hemispheric processes, the heavy emphasis upon the three Rs (left hemisphere) in our educational system tends to neglect the right hemisphere. Deliberate exercises in mental imagery appear to be a simple and direct way of creating a better balance and harmony between the left and right hemispheres of the brain.

Here are some imagery exercises that many psychologists prescribe for achieving "brain synchrony" or "mental harmony." You can readily test out these exercises for yourself and see whether they truly assist you in developing both greater energy and serenity.

BRAIN SYNCHRONY EXERCISES

Exercise 1. The Blackboard

Sit down in a comfortable manner in a quiet place. Take several deep breaths and relax. Now close your eyes and imagine a blackboard and picture yourself writing the letter "A" on the board. Now add the letter "B" and keep adding letters. Some people can complete the entire alphabet in this way. See how far along *you* can get. As you keep adding letters, what happens? Do some of them fade away? Do they become hazy? Examine your own pattern, and each time you do this exercise, try to obtain more and more clarity. A five-minute practice session is sufficient.

Exercise 2. The Light Bulb

Close your eyes and imagine a dim light bulb suspended in front of you. As you keep imagining the light, see if you can make it grow brighter and dimmer in your mind's eye. Alternate between brightness and dimness. Now imagine the light growing brighter, and brighter. See if you can let it become so bright that it illuminates everything. Then little by little, let it grow less and less bright, until it once again becomes a dim light bulb suspended in front of you. Again, a total of about five minutes of practice time is sufficient.

Exercise 3. The Common Object

Take any common object, *a real object,* any handy item, and examine it carefully. (You can look at any object—a stone, a piece of fruit, a bottle, a pencil, a watch, anything available.) Keep looking directly at the object until you are very familiar with it. Study it closely. Now close your eyes and imagine that you are still looking directly at the object. Picture it as clearly as you can. Study the image as you did when you were examining the real object. Keep picturing the object. Now open your eyes. Re-examine the real object. Compare the difference between the image and the actual object. Look closely at the object to see if there are any features that you did not register in the image. Close your eyes again and repeat the exercise.

Exercise 4. The Seashore

Get comfortable, relax, close your eyes, and imagine that you are on a quiet beach on a warm sunny day. You are wearing a swim suit and you are strolling along the beach. Feel the warm sand between your toes. Also feel the pleasantly warm sun. Take in a deep breath and smell the fresh sea air. Become aware of the sun again, see the sky and the waves. Go to the water's edge and wade up to your ankles. Feel the cool water. Try to feel a pleasant breeze. Notice how the air feels on your skin. Hear the waves breaking on the shore. Now imagine yourself walking quickly on the sand. Feel your muscles stretching. Walk past a hot dog stand and smell the aroma of food. Try to enjoy it. Sit under an umbrella looking out to sea. See the shimmering light dancing on the water, watch the breakers roll in, and feel the calm sensations that accompany this image.

While I am not aware of any controlled studies demonstrating that these exercises result in more harmonious left-brain/right-brain functioning, a number of theorists and practitioners are convinced that they have a most beneficial effect. I find that these imagery exercises elicit a feeling of calmness combined with energy. One of my patients claims that exercises 3 and 4 make her feel tranquil and peaceful, whereas exercises 1 and 2 produce a sense of personal mastery and a feeling of self-confidence. You might care to spend about five to ten minutes each morning and evening on these exercises and see if they make you feel generally more calm, more energetic, and less excitable.

It is important to stress that the use of imagery is not new in psychotherapy. French, German, and Italian practitioners have applied ingenious imagery techniques for the past twenty-five years. The famous Swiss professor, C. G. Jung, made extensive use of what he termed "active imagination," in which patients are asked to re-dream specific dreams in the consulting room by re-experiencing them in imagination. In the past, European psychotherapists have tended to show greater interest in imagery than American clinicians, but in the U.S.A. there has been a recent upsurge of interest in the therapeutic use of imagery techniques. In fact most of the methods discussed in this book stem from research conducted in America.

Once more, let us discuss how vivid or clear the various images need to be in order to achieve the desired results. Some people can readily and rapidly picture real or fictitious scenes without difficulty. Others have to concentrate for a while before conjuring up an image, and even then they may find that their images are somewhat hazy. There are some individuals who can examine a picture, project their image of it onto a blank wall or a screen, and then behave as if they were still actually seeing the picture by describing it in great detail. This type of photographic clarity is called *eidetic* imagery. It is fairly common in children, but rare in adults. Let it be understood that when referring to imagery throughout this book, we are *not* talking about eidetic imagery. While the more vivid the image, the better the result, it is sufficient merely to recall the required images in the mind's eye.

Thus, if I ask you to picture the living room in your childhood home you need not achieve the clarity you would obtain from an actual photograph. Simply remember how it looked, and focus on that memory. That level of imagery is quite sufficient for our purposes. You might also remember that very few people can maintain a total image. For instance, when visualizing a car, we "see" fenders, bumpers, light, or wheels, but we rarely see it all together—as we focus on an image, various parts may come and go.

Imagery techniques are used in many areas of mental training. For example, most memory teachers evoke imagery as an aid in remembering unrelated items. Expert mnemonists use precise (sometimes deliberately bizarre) images to facilitate the recall of names, faces, places, words, numbers, and so forth. The well-known memory trainer Harry Lorayne advises his pupils to conjure up mental images or pictures that link together words, objects, etc. Using the *link technique,* one successively associates numerous items by making the associations as illogical and as ridiculous as possible. These very strange links are then visualized in a mental picture.

For example, if someone is asked to memorize a long list of unrelated words such as "car," "hot dog," "telephone," "elephant," "suitcase," "house," "candy bar," and so forth, a mnemonic image would be the following. Starting with the *car,* one would picture a *hot dog* sticking out from the windshield, with a roll shaped like a *telephone* all on top of an *elephant* with a *suitcase* in its trunk, standing on the roof of a *house* made out of *candy bars.* The image can grow more and more ridiculous (and therefore easier to remember) as additional words are added to the list. In this way, experts can memorize or recall dozens of words, items, numbers, or what have you.

In this book we use imagery quite differently. Our aim is to employ imagery to control negative emotions and to overcome undesirable behaviors. We are also interested in the power of imagery for promoting social skills and for achieving personal mastery. Goal rehearsal is one of the most versatile mental imagery techniques. It is a method of *practicing in the mind* the specific goals one wishes to attain. With the use of goal rehearsal, practice may be said to make the improbable quite feasible! The next chapter describes this important process.

PART II

Using Imagery to Build Confidence and Skill

CHAPTER 4

Goal Rehearsal to Build Confidence and Skill

Watching television and films is perhaps one of the most literal forms of imagery. Motion pictures, as most people know, are a series of individual images projected in rapid succession, with each image depicting a slight change, thereby producing the optical effect of a continuous picture with the illusion of movement.

The impact of these images, especially on children, is considered to be most significant. For instance, much has been written and debated about the results of violence on television. There is evidence that criminal tendencies can be fostered by certain programs.

On the positive side, there are studies showing that children, even of pre-school age, can be taught a variety of useful skills by motion pictures. This includes teaching them how to use cooperative rather than aggressive behaviors, how to change social withdrawal into constructive social interaction, and how to overcome various fears. The child sees films of his peers behaving in non-disruptive ways and observes them receiving various rewards for so doing. Very often, the viewer then copies or models what was depicted on film, and thus several useful social responses are learned in place of formerly self-defeating habits and behaviors.

Dr. Albert Bandura and his associates at Stanford University have carried out controlled studies in the area of symbolic modeling. For example, they treated children who were extremely afraid of dogs. The phobic children were helped very rapidly by seeing movies in which other children played enjoyably with dogs and did not get harmed. Even adults respond to this type of emotional retraining.

People with snake phobias saw films of adults and children handling snakes, enjoying themselves in the process, coming to no harm, and generally having obvious fun with the snakes. This was quite effective in ridding several people of their snake phobias. These studies show how effective the process of imitation tends to be. Fortunately, we do not have to rely on movies in order to harness the positive effects of imitation. Our images are quite sufficient for this purpose, as the rest of this chapter will illustrate.

EXAGGERATED ROLE-TAKING (FOR OVERCOMING TENSION OR ANXIETY)

The significance of *imitation* can hardly be overstated. We all learn many things in life by imitating others, especially those whom we respect and admire. In 1966 I described the use of a technique called *exaggerated role-taking*. Here, one pictures somebody else coping easily and effortlessly with a situation that would ordinarily prove difficult for him or her. One then imitates the successful person's actions. As an illustration, a woman mentioned that she was constantly blowing up at her 7-year-old daughter. Whenever the child misbehaved, the mother would become tense, over-react, berate the child, and scold her vehemently. The child would cry, and soon the mother would be consumed by guilt. "How can I stop myself from behaving so foolishly?" she asked me. "I have promised myself dozens of times to start treating my daughter differently, but I don't seem to have enough patience and self-control when it comes down to it." I recommended the use of exaggerated role-taking.

First the mother and I carefully examined the behavior traits that she valued and wished to emulate. Next I asked her to think of someone who possessed these traits. She had a friend whom she considered elegant, graceful, self-contained, dignified, confident, and refined. "When your child next misbehaves," I suggested, "immediately picture that gracious and graceful woman and imagine how she would deal with your daughter. Would she raise her voice? Of course not! Would she lose her temper? Never! You can very quickly assess how she would respond, you can see it in your mind's eye. *And then go right ahead and imitate her.*" She found that the exaggerated role enabled her to achieve self-control and helped her become more patient and less irascible.

One can practice the foregoing scene in advance of any actual confrontations. Thus the mother, while sitting and relaxing quietly at home, can picture her daughter acting in an annoying fashion, and then she can imagine herself (or see the ideal mother) handling her daughter helpfully and constructively. This particular scene is rehearsed several times so that when it actually occurs, one is ready for it, and the newfound desirable behaviors can be brought into play.

There are, of course, degrees of exaggeration. For example, a rather plain young girl who was nervous about going out on a date with an especially attractive man was advised to imagine that she was actually a princess incognita who had condescended to go out with a commoner. She was to keep this image firmly in mind and to keep repeating silently to herself, "I am a princess, you are a commoner," when she felt tense or nervous. She had a vivid imagination and carried out her assignment to the letter. "My fears vanished after a few minutes," she said, "and then I simply dropped the role and had a good time."

A young man who was extremely uncomfortable about returning unsuitable or damaged merchandise to stores used exaggerated role-taking most effectively. "I remember a story about a billionaire who would buy hotels, restaurants, or shops where he had been offended by sales people so that he, as the new owner, could fire them. I bought a new suit, had it pinned for alteration, but when it was delivered altered and I tried it on at home it fitted very poorly. So I pretended to myself that I was worth millions of dollars and that I nevertheless wanted my money's worth, or else I would buy out the owner and dismiss his tailor. I imagined the way such a wealthy person would think and feel, and then I went back to the store and expressed my displeasure. It was easy on my nerves and I also seemed to command respect. I ended up with a suit that fits perfectly.''

There are many applications of this technique, and the enterprising reader will undoubtedly be able to apply exaggerated role-taking to several situations and rapidly test out the effectiveness of this procedure. Exaggerated role-taking is especially helpful whenever you are with people who make you feel nervous, inferior, or uncomfortable. Try to imagine yourself as someone very powerful and important and play the part to the hilt. Business-related situations are the most frequent avenues for using this technique. Employees who feel intimidated by their employers are obvious candidates for this method.

Many writers are now pointing out that women who wish to proceed up the management ladder are at a special disadvantage. They have been conditioned to avoid taking risks; they tend to have little confidence in being able to control their own fates; and often they allow others to define what they should and ought to be. Thus, women even more than men, need to rehearse in their mind's eye exactly how to go about asking for a raise, handling a put-down, dealing with a competitor, speaking out at a meeting, and being appropriately assertive when treated unfairly. The essence of the role-taking method is first to decide exactly what would be an appropriate response in a given situation. One may arrive at this by discussing matters with friends and associates, or simply by making up one's own mind on the subject. Thereafter, over and over again, one relaxes and clearly imagines oneself engaging in the desired behavior. One may then elect to add the exaggeration component in order to feel more self-assured. As one young woman discovered when dealing with chauvinistic males at a sales meeting, if she pictured herself possessing a concealed weapon that could instantly obliterate anyone in the room, she immediately felt self-confident and was then able to conduct herself in the assertive manner that she had so often practiced in her imagery exercises. Let us discuss other illustrations of imagery applied to business and work-related situations.

IMAGERY ON THE JOB

Practically everyone who has an upcoming interview for a new job will tend to rehearse in his or her mind the various questions that are likely to be asked, and the best answers that one can provide. Instead of the vague and general rehearsals that most people employ, I am recommending that some time be spent conjuring up a vivid image of an interview situation. I am advocating that a deliberate and very detailed scene be enacted in the mind. Use different images. In one of them, see yourself being introduced to the interviewer; in another scene, see yourself taking the initiative and making a self-introduction. Picture yourself being asked background questions, and after rehearsing your answers, try to see yourself looking cool and confident. As vividly as possible, picture yourself sitting in a relaxed manner, walking and talking in a self-assured and calm fashion. The more these mental images are practiced, the greater the likelihood that they will spill over into the actual interview.

In my own day-to-day interactions, I have found various situations in which it is difficult to be cheerful. For example, while grading class tests or examinations, while attending long-drawn-out committee meetings, or while answering routine correspondence, many people are likely to become bored or disgruntled rather than cheerful. I seem to have a particularly low threshold for these situations, but since they are a necessary part of my university work I decided to test out the power of imagery. I simply pictured myself feeling cheerful in each of these situations. Several times a day over the course of a few weeks, I would see myself engaged in routine chores and I would deliberately inject an aura of cheerfulness into the image. An interesting thing happened. My mind had to find something to be cheerful about, something legitimate; after all, there is little intrinsically cheerful about a dull meeting or a poorly written examination. However, when I would introduce cheerfulness into a dull image, it would change automatically. It would begin with me sitting and feeling very bored, and then I would manage to say or do something in the image that would remedy the situation. For instance, in a never-ending committee meeting, I would see myself suggesting a ten-minute recess, or I would picture myself coming up with a suggestion that would soon put an end to this meeting. When grading an uninspiring examination, I would see myself writing marginal comments that would be helpful to the student. Thus, the cheerful image transformed *how-can-I-g e t -through-reading-this-dull-examination* into *h o w -c a n -I -u se-this-as-a-vehicle-for-teaching-the-student?* The upshot is that committee meetings and marking examinations have taken on a different (more pleasant) meaning for me. There has been a decided shift in attitude.

One of the most relevant applications of imagery on the job concerns people who sell for a living (real estate, life insurance, and the like). Success at selling can be enhanced by rehearsing every angle in the mind's eye. For example, one of my friends, a manufacturer, was introducing a new golf bag onto the market. I asked why people would buy his bag rather than well-established brand names such as Arnold Palmer. He replied: "Because I have gone over every possible objection in my own mind and I have come up with clear-cut answers. I have even pictured myself persuading Arnold Palmer to buy my golf bag!" Suffice it to say that over the years my friend has sold thousands of his golf bags (and a wide variety of other leather goods). Let me re-emphasize the basic dictum: *If you repeatedly and conscientiously picture yourself achieving a goal, your chances of actual success will be greatly enhanced.*

GOAL REHEARSAL

Some years ago, when applying for a job that I wanted very much, I clearly visualized what it would be like to get the position. I pictured myself in that particular setting and felt more excited and optimistic about the prospect. But I could also see myself not getting the job, and I deliberately pictured myself being normally disappointed (not neurotically crushed or depressed). I then pictured myself exploring other work outlets. In this instance, I did not get the job, felt disappointed, but knew exactly how to cope (because I had rehearsed several alternatives). As so often happens, I ended up getting a far better job in the end.

Let us turn to a case study in which the use of goal rehearsal enabled a young man to stand up to his overbearing father (who was also his employer).

Case Study

Many people suffer needlessly because they fail to assert their basic rights. Instead of speaking their minds, expressing their frank opinions, and refusing to accede to unreasonable requests, timid and frightened people are more apt to stifle their feelings and conform to the needs of others. Often, they stew in their own resentment and lose self-respect. Goal re-

61

hearsal facilitates the achievement of self-confidence. One practices saying "no" to unreasonable requests, expressing negative feelings, asking for favors, or simply making requests. One pictures the settings and events as vividly as possible, and very deliberately and realistically, a dialogue is enacted in imagination. Generally, one draws a clear line between assertion and aggression, but with some people it is necessary to overstep one's assertive prerogatives.

For example, a 25-year-old man worked in his father's business. The father was a powerful, dictatorial individual who shouted down any new ideas his son tried to introduce. At my instigation, the son practiced goal rehearsal. He imagined suggesting to his father that a new line of merchandise be introduced. He would then picture his father's typical reaction—ranting and raving. I instructed the son to keep picturing the image, to keep on trying to find a way to get through to his father in the image. It took him more than a week of imagery practice to picture himself outdoing his father's tirade. In his mind's eye he saw himself banging the desk with his fist and yelling, "The only way to get heard in this place is to yell louder than you can." In real life, the son was inclined to be quiet and withdrawn and he had never raised his voice to his father. I encouraged him to act out his fantasy. "I can't do it!" he protested. This is where goal rehearsal came into force. I asked him to rehearse in his mind the shouting scene over and over again.

It took yet another week, during which time the

son pictured himself outdoing his father's vitupera-
tion hundreds and hundreds of times. He rehearsed
this image so thoroughly that it began to feel like
second nature to him. Two days later he called me to
report that it had been put to good use. "My dad
was yelling and carrying on and quite suddenly, almost by complete surprise, it came out of me. . . .
Just as I had done so many times in my image I
pounded the desk, and shouted at the top of my lungs
that I was sick of being treated like a child, sick of
being yelled at, sick of being overruled. . . . My
father was nonplussed. . . . For the first time in my
life, as far back as I can remember, my dad backed
down and gave in to me." As the reader can well
imagine, the upshot of this interaction was a new-
found respect between father and son, and a greater
feeling of self-confidence in a formerly timid and inhibited young man.

ASSERTIVE BEHAVIOR

An example of goal rehearsal in the acquisition of
assertive (not *aggressive*) behavior concerned a female nurse whose immediate superior was a male
doctor who was arrogant, chauvinistic, condescend-
ing, and inconsiderate. She had endeavored to express her discontent on several occasions, but she
inevitably became tearful when she began confront-
ing him, and thereby only felt foolish and doubly
inept.

I advised her to practice a clear and concise
imaginary confrontation over and over again for at

least ten days before venturing to approach him again. She was to relax, close her eyes, and visualize herself telling the doctor off—assertively, not aggressively—without getting upset. A prepared script was specially composed for the occasion.

"Dr. Smithers, I would like a few minutes of your time to share some important personal observations with you. Let me get straight to the point. I do not enjoy working with you. While I respect your medical knowledge and believe that you are a fine physician, I find your attitude toward me patronizing and humiliating. Frankly, I am not alone in this opinion, and I think it detracts from your overall effectiveness as a doctor and as a human being."

She memorized this speech and pictured herself saying it to the doctor. To be certain that her feelings would be positive, regardless of his response, I had her picture several negative outcomes. In one imagined scene the doctor reacted angrily and snapped at her, "When I want your opinion I'll ask for it!" In another scene he became even more pompous and sneering, greeting her final line with mocking laughter while walking away. She was to picture these negative outcomes, but to continue to see herself unruffled.

After almost two weeks of daily goal rehearsals, she finally took the risk of carrying out her assignment. Morning ward rounds had been completed and they were alone in the nurses' station when she approached him. He heard her out, and said that he had no idea she felt so negatively toward him. He then invited her to have lunch with him so that they could "come to terms." The situation was then very adequately settled.

If one of the negative outcomes had come to pass, we would have rehearsed a different script, emphasizing the need for her to transfer to another unit of the hospital. If this proved impossible, two other immediate solutions would have been (a) to desensitize her to the doctor's patronizing attitude (see Chapter 5), or (b) to employ goal rehearsal in applying successfully for another job.

For instance, she would think of other hospitals where she might like to work; she would carefully scan professional journals for job opportunities; she would respond to selected advertisements; she would picture herself asking friends and associates if they knew of job openings; she would systematically rehearse job interviews before exposing herself to the actual situations and would visualize what to say and how to say it once in the interview.

There are innumerable interpersonal situations in which the use of goal rehearsal can prove extremely helpful. Most people will rehearse dialogues in their minds before an important meeting or in anticipation of a significant encounter. But few people take these imaginary conversations far enough. They do not rehearse the scenes clearly and thoroughly and therefore often find themselves at a loss for words. For example, a woman who was going through an unpleasant divorce was expecting a phone call from her estranged husband regarding a property settlement. Before the phone call she imagined how the conversation would go, and she rehearsed the way in which she would insist on certain rights. But she failed to rehearse several different tactics in case her husband proved uncooperative (which was most probable). She had falsely assumed that things would go her way. In the end, the phone call was mismanaged because she was not able to counter his maneuvers, and she emerged feeling somewhat cheated. Yet it would have been relatively simple for her to have predicted his reactions and to have been ready with effective arguments and counter-arguments. She would have been well-advised to prepare several different scripts before the phone call.

People who attach great value to spontaneity may be appalled at the thought of sitting down and writing out their own scripts. If one is particularly quick-witted and can interject replies and return comments with deft repartee, the labor of preparing detailed notes can be safely circumvented. But many people who rely on their spontaneity merely improvise themselves into tight corners. Scripts, carefully written out and prepared in advance, are especially valuable in dealing with difficult telephone conversations.

GOAL REHEARSAL FOR ENHANCING ATHLETIC PERFORMANCE

Mental imagery provides the opportunity to practice many new skills and to develop different attitudes and traits. Naturally a real event differs considerably from one that is merely being imagined.

However, there are a sufficient number of neurones (nerve endings) in common between those affected in the actual situation and those affected by one's image of that situation, so that reciprocal interaction takes place. In other words, neuro-physiologically, if you look at a pencil, the nerve pathways from your eyes to your brain and your central nervous system enable you to register the meaning, the perception, and the experience of seeing the pencil. Now if you close your eyes and imagine the pencil as vividly as possible, the image of the pencil will stimulate many thousands of the same neurones that were involved when registering the actual pencil. Thus, if you picture yourself behaving or performing in a certain manner, it will overlap with your performance in the real situation. *Fortis imaginatio generat causum* (A strong imagination generates the actual event).

Studies have shown that if a golfer imagines himself driving a ball or making a difficult putt over and over again, his actual game will improve. Similarly, the mental practice of picturing oneself successfully throwing darts at a target will improve one's aim in the real situation. This applies to nearly all specific skills. *If you practice something in imagination, it is bound to have an effect on the real situation.* Everybody knows this and probably uses it from time to time, but we are advocating a deliberate and systematic excursion into "goal rehearsal" in order to facilitate numerous skills.

One of my patients, a champion tennis player, was due to play in a tournament in six weeks. However, he was also a medical student and was scheduled to spend those six weeks on an intensive inpatient training rotation. He was therefore unable to train for his match and might, at best, have managed to get in two or three sets of tennis during those critical six weeks. He considered withdrawing from the tournament. I advised him to use goal rehearsal. Several times each day for a minute or two at a time, he was to relax, close his eyes, and vividly picture himself executing various shots on the tennis court. He practiced his serve, backhand, dropshots, top spin, etc., purely *in his imagination*. Although he was skeptical about the real-life transfer, I encouraged him to continue practicing the images. To his surprise, when he finally played in the tournament after six weeks of goal rehearsal, his game was better than ever. I recall his expression of astonishment when he said, "It really works!"

In a recent radio interview, Chris Evert was asked how she practiced for a championship match. She stated that in addition to actual practice she carefully and painstakingly tended to rehearse every significant detail of an upcoming match *in her mind's eye*. She thinks about her opponent's style and form, and she visualizes herself countering each and every maneuver that person may make during the match.

Dr. Richard Suinn of Colorado State University has conducted scientific studies on the use of goal rehearsal to improve the skills of athletes. As a consultant to the U.S. National Olympic Ski Team, he has skiers relaxing and then imagining the actual race. The skiers see themselves at the top of the course just before the start of an event. They then traverse the entire slope in imagery. Many of the skiers find the imagery so real that they experience most of the sensations they would have in actual competition. There is the wind in his face, the crunch of snow under his skis, his feet turning in the direction he imagines skiing, and his muscles twitching from the effort. The value of this type of training has become quite evident. Dr. Michael Mahoney of Pennsylvania State University has also conducted studies on the use of mental imagery for improving athletic performance. Again, the outcomes point to goal rehearsal as a powerful adjunct to regular training.

This is not to minimize the importance of actual practice. To claim that it is unnecessary to perform actual tasks but that the mere imagined rehearsal will guarantee mastery is absurd. But when discussing training methods with successful athletes, I have noticed that the majority employ some form of goal rehearsal in addition to their overt training. And I am claiming that if you are already good at something, the practice of goal rehearsal can make you even better. I mentioned the foregoing to a young man who plays basketball. He decided to give goal rehearsal a try. At various free moments during the day, and before falling asleep at night, he would imagine himself throwing the ball through the net. After only one week he claimed that goal rehearsal had improved his accuracy by more than sixty percent.

There are many applications of goal rehearsal. For example, it may pay you to display more warmth and friendship toward other people, at home and at work. If that image—acting more friendly— is rehearsed, it becomes a *fait accompli*.

In this instance you would need to see exactly what it means for you to be more friendly. You would picture yourself greeting more people, smiling at them, asking friendly questions, paying compliments, displaying interest, expressing thanks or gratitude when appropriate, and ending conversations with statements such as, "I look forward to seeing you soon," or "Have a nice day." Shy people usually feel very awkward when engaging in these pleasantries. Goal rehearsal will encourage them to feel far more at ease during these perfunctory interchanges, and they will derive two distinct benefits: (1) Other people will no longer view them as shy or unfriendly, and (2) they, in turn, will develop a much greater feeling of self-assurance and social skill.

In the same way, if a pessimist practices picturing optimistic outcomes and incidents, a decided and positive shift in outlook will be achieved. Many people believe that pessimism protects them from being disappointed. "I always assume that things are going to go wrong, and in that way, when things do go wrong, I am ready for it because I expected it." This is a dangerous philosophy because it is likely to become a self-fulfilling prophecy. If you assume that things will go wrong, you may inadvertently aid and abet the negative outcome. The wise course is to picture yourself achieving and enjoying

70

positive outcomes, but you can always insure your-self against negative outcomes by also viewing your-self exploring *other viable options* if and when events do happen to go wrong.

Let us examine two additional applications of goal rehearsal techniques.

STAGE FRIGHT

There is a large amount of clinical and experimental evidence which shows that goal rehearsal facilitates live performance. I was consulted by a well-known and talented actress, who tended to get "stage fright" from time to time and was losing self-confi-dence. Before seeing me, she had been to two psy-chiatrists, both of whom had imputed hidden motives to her fears. They believed that she had an unconscious desire to fail as an actress, and that only years of psychoanalysis would enable her to overcome her fears. She was most unhappy at the prospect of spending years being psychoanalyzed, and she therefore made inquiries about other methods of therapy. She was then referred to me.

Instead of delving into her so-called uncon-scious mind, I advised her to practice goal rehearsal. Several times a day, each and every day without fail, she was to relax, and then to picture herself on stage. But for the purposes of goal rehearsal she was to see herself on stage as the most self-assured, self-confident, and dynamic actress that ever lived. Thus, by combining the natural practice effect of goal rehearsal with exaggerated role-taking in her fantasy, I believed that a large part of the very positive mental image would transfer to her actual performance. And indeed this took place. After seeing herself, day after day, in image after image, on stage, acting brilliantly, bringing the audience to their feet with enthusiastic applause, her actual performances began to approximate some of her more fanciful fantasies. Instead of requiring years of psychoanalysis, goal rehearsal accomplished its aim in less than a month and a half.

Let it be understood that I am not claiming that a little (or even a lot) of goal rehearsal can make great actors or actresses out of anyone. What I am claiming is that the deliberate practice of goal rehearsal can maximize and actualize whatever potential talents and abilities lie dormant in a person. And everyone has the capacity to be happier, more relaxed, more self-accepting, more confident, and more effective in their dealings with other people in innumerable contexts.

SEXUAL DYSFUNCTIONS

Another area in which goal rehearsal has proved to be especially useful is that of sexual dysfunction. I have successfully treated many so-called frigid or non-orgasmic women by means of goal rehearsal. Again, in this homework assignment, the woman deliberately relaxes several times a day, and pictures herself enjoyably engaged in sexual intercourse. If she attaches a fairly high level of anxiety to sexual participation, one would first employ a desensitization procedure (see Chapter 5). I have found that when a woman is able to imagine herself enjoyably and passionately engaged in sexual relations, a positive transfer to the actual lovemaking soon follows. The same is often true of impotent men.

If men rehearse scenes in which they see themselves engaged in erotic or passionate sexual encounters, there is usually a transfer of sexual potency to the real-life situation. An important finding is that masturbation fantasies usually do not produce sexual potency in the real-life sexual situation. Goal rehearsal of sexual potency needs to be practiced during periods of *non-arousal*. One relaxes and distinctly pictures eminently positive and potent lovemaking scenes in which the person clearly sees himself performing adequately. The man with erection difficulties needs to experience himself, in his mind's eye, having no sexual difficulties whatsoever. Here is a basic rule: *If you wish to accomplish something in reality, first picture yourself achieving it in imagination.*

Dr. Gerald Davison of State University of New York at Stony Brook has used imagery extensively, both experimentally and clinically. He combined rehearsal and aversive imagery in a particularly interesting case of sexual deviance. A young man was greatly troubled by an obsessive sexual fantasy—he found great (if not sole) sexual stimulation in imagining an attractive woman tied to stakes in the ground while tearfully trying to extricate herself. He had masturbated to this sadistic fantasy for a period of ten years, and was anxious to rid himself of this image. He wanted to be able to be aroused by women without having to conjure up this hostile image.

Dr. Davison employed a variety of associated images, but his principal strategy was to instruct the young man to masturbate to actual pictures of provocative and untied nude women, and to generate a disturbing and nauseating image when he conjured up the sadistic fantasy. Davison carefully arranged the time sequence so that sadistic fantasies faded because they were associated with the nauseating image, while ordinary heterosexual fantasies became invested with a high degree of sexual arousal and excitement. At the end of this treatment, a woman's body became the sexual stimulus, and no hostile or sadistic fantasies entered the young man's mind.

The powers of goal rehearsal are difficult to overstate. When people see themselves achieving things they wish to achieve, and when they rehearse these images over and over, week after week, month after month, the probability of reaching their perceived goals becomes more and more likely. But many problems can block one's path—fears and phobias, undesirable habits, negative emotions, psychosomatic disorders, even "future shock." The rest of this book will show you how to use imagery to eradicate each one of these potential barriers and frustrations.

CHAPTER 5

Overcoming Adult Fears and Anxieties with Imagery Techniques

A phobia is an irrational fear of a harmless object or situation. The word "phobia" is derived from the Greek *phobos* which means fright, terror, or panic. Phobos was a mythical Greek god who would provoke fear and trembling in one's enemies. The phobic sufferer is usually fully aware that his or her fear is ridiculous and without foundation, and yet the unreasonable fear persists. People realize that their phobias are out of proportion to the real event, but they cannot reason them away and almost always avoid their feared situations.

Numerous Greek and Latin prefixes have been attached to the word phobia to describe a variety of specific fears. Thus, people who fear animals are said to have zoöphobia. A morbid fear of spiders is arachnophobia (from the Greek *arakhne*, meaning spider). A fear of heights is acrophobia. Aquaphobia means water phobia. A fear of lightning is astraphobia. A fear of closed spaces is claustrophobia (from the Latin *claustrum,* which means to cloister or confine). Many people suffer from *agoraphobia* (literally, a fear of the marketplace). These people fear open spaces, being alone, or traveling anywhere on their own. It is possible for people to develop phobias to an amazingly vast range of stimuli.

There is not much agreement on the way in which people acquire fears and phobias. Some authorities view them as symbolic representations of underlying conflicts. Thus, a fear of sharp objects may really mask hidden aggression. Other experts regard phobias as the result of negative associations or conditioning. In other words, they assume that some frightening events can cause long-lasting sensitivities. Hence, after being stuck in an elevator for several hours, a person might become claustrophobic, avoiding going into elevators and also keeping out of all closed-in places. If the original mishap in the elevator was in a large department store, the person might also avoid large shops. Indeed, the fear might generalize even further, so that the person now avoids elevators, department stores, moving vehicles, public gatherings, and many other situations. However, contrary to popular opinion, it is not important to understand the basic mechanisms and dynamics in order to overcome phobic reactions.

Many phobic individuals often obtain secondary gains from their disabilities—that is, some form of attention or other benefit as a result of the problem.

For example, let us assume that the above-mentioned claustrophobic is a woman whose husband now does all the shopping and who pays undue attention to his frightened little wife, who enjoys being pampered. One can readily appreciate how and why the woman's phobias are being maintained. Obviously, not all cases are that clear-cut. However, if you suffer from phobias, and if you genuinely want to overcome them, the first step is to take a hard and deeply honest look at possible secondary gains that you (and others) might be deriving. It is extremely difficult to overcome a phobia without first discarding the secondary gains.

Nevertheless, not all phobic sufferers obtain secondary gains. Many people are afraid of certain things, places, situations, or events, and they have no doubts whatsoever about wishing to rid themselves of these fears. What constructive steps can they take?

SYSTEMATIC DESENSITIZATION

In 1955 as a graduate student of psychology, in Johannesburg, South Africa, I was taught a technique called "systematic desensitization" by Dr. Joseph Wolpe, now Professor of Psychiatry at Temple University School of Medicine. This method for overcoming phobias consists of three separate steps. (1) The client is shown how to relax the major muscles in his or her body, so that a state of calm and serenity prevails. It should be pointed out that the art of deep muscle relaxation has profound effects when practiced regularly and systematically.* Initially, we employed hypnosis, but we soon learned that relaxation is better because it does not make the patient dependent. Relaxation also provides a useful skill that one can apply in many normally tense situations. (2) The phobia is broken up into a series of steps. For example, if the person is afraid of hospitals, we would probably start with items such as seeing a sign that said "hospital," seeing a hospital way off in the distance, driving past a hospital. More and more difficult items would be added to the list, such as sitting in the lobby of a hospital, seeing a patient being wheeled past on a stretcher, smelling the usual hospital odors. Finally, the most fearful items might include seeing patients coming out of surgery, seeing a friend in the intensive care unit, being in a large surgical ward. (3) When the patient has gained some proficiency at relaxation (and this usually takes most people a couple of weeks of daily relaxation training), he or she is systematically asked to picture each item on the list of fears.

One begins by visualizing the easiest item. "Imagine that you are having a pleasant outing with some friends, and you drive past a sign that says 'Hospital. Next Right Turn'." While relaxed, the person pictures this scene as vividly as possible. If this easy scene arouses anxiety, one may have to commence with something even less upsetting, such as perhaps having fun at a hospital fete or bazaar. Each successive item on the list is presented to the

* Two different types of relaxation training scripts are included in the appendix.

imagination again and again, until it no longer proves at all disturbing. As each item is nullified, the next item is presented. Usually, only a few weeks of desensitization are required before the person can picture the most disturbing item without experiencing subjective discomfort. And in most cases the person is then able to enter the actual feared situation without experiencing the former anxiety.

Practically everybody has at least one phobialike sensitivity. For example, *social phobias* are most prominent because so many people are deeply concerned about public opinion. The fear of humiliation is pre-eminent, and this over-riding fear ties in with hypersensitivities to criticism, rejection, and disapproval. Many of us may have no particular fear of heights or confined spaces or spiders or blood or snakes, etc., but we may over-react to arguments, avoid asking questions in class, creep into our shell at a party, or be petrified when called upon to make a speech. These types of social anxieties may be viewed as phobias, and treated accordingly. Ask yourself, "What specific hypersensitivities do I have?" "What sorts of situations do I painstakingly avoid?" Perhaps you shy away from social gatherings, or you avoid asking for favors, or going out on dates, or speaking in public, or perhaps you give in too easily and do other people's dirty work because you avoid saying "No!" and you avoid standing up for your rights. Whatever your own particular areas of avoidance happen to be, you might be well advised to use one of the methods outlined below.

A majority of my patients are unduly self-conscious, terrified of failure, and preoccupied with fears of disapproval, rejection, criticism, and loss of respect. The desensitization procedure is often the most effective way of ridding them of these hypersensitivities. The procedure is the same as that for a clear-cut phobia. Recently, I treated a young man with a phobia of eating in public places. He was most comfortable when eating alone at home, somewhat less comfortable when his parents were at the table, even more uncomfortable when a male friend was present, but by far the worst situation was eating in the company of an attractive young woman, which was the goal he wanted to reach. He drew up the following list:

1. Having lunch alone at the table with my parents in the other room.
2. Having breakfast with my father at the table.
3. Having dinner at home with both of my parents.
4. Having breakfast alone in an empty cafeteria.
5. Having breakfast alone at a cafeteria with a few other people at different tables.
6. Having dinner with my parents at home together with one of their friends.
7. Having dinner with a male friend in his apartment.
8. Having dinner at an old friend's house, with his parents.

9. Having dinner in an empty restaurant with an unattractive female.

10. Having lunch at the University cafeteria with three classmates.

11. Having dinner at my friend's house with him, his parents, and his fairly attractive girlfriend.

12. Having breakfast out with an attractive woman.

13. Having dinner out with an attractive woman.

14. Having dinner at an attractive girlfriend's house, with several people, including her parents.

As he relaxed deeply and pictured each item, one by one, he experienced considerable anticipatory anxiety when we reached item number 5. I made him switch off the scene, concentrate on achieving even deeper levels of relaxation, and presented item number 5 again and again, until he felt absolutely no discomfort.

Item number 9 (having dinner in an empty restaurant with an unattractive female) triggered a surprisingly high level of initial anxiety. Here again, we had to withdraw the scene from his imagination and increase his feelings of calmness, serenity, and peaceful relaxation. Thereafter, we easily covered the next three items, and encountered some expected difficulty with item number 13 (having dinner out with an attractive woman). However, the entire list of fourteen items was covered in seven sessions during three and a half weeks, whereupon he celebrated by taking out a most attractive woman and several other friends to an expensive restaurant.

The procedure of desensitization through imagery is based on a very significant assumption. *The things we fear in reality, we also fear in imagination.* The corollary is that *the things we no longer fear in imagination will also not disturb us in the actual situation.* These rules seem to apply to most people. In psychology, few rules apply to all people. Some individuals can picture their feared situations and experience no anxiety whatsoever, but the moment they are confronted by the actual stimuli, terror automatically takes over. These people will probably need to expose themselves to their actual fears in a stepwise or piecemeal fashion. Fortunately, however, the majority of people can conquer all sorts of fears by the use of mental imagery.

SELF-DESENSITIZATION

A number of therapists have obtained good results by teaching their patients how to desensitize themselves. It is not difficult to achieve a sufficient degree of relaxation to offset minor anxieties. In the privacy of one's own home, and entirely at one's own convenience, it is possible to draw up a personal list of fears and phobias, and to overcome each item one by one. For months after lecturing about self-desensitization at a public meeting, I received letters from people who had applied the method successfully. Here is a typical example:

*I used to be terribly afraid of seeing cripples
or blind people. Seeing anyone on crutches, in
a wheelchair, with a missing limb, or with any
deformity, would make me feel quite anxious.
If I could not remove myself immediately, I
would often start to feel ill. I used your cassette on relaxation for about ten days and
then I relaxed myself without the cassette
and imagined some less frightening scenes. For
example, there is a blind man who always sits
with his dog outside a shoe store in my neighborhood. I had always crossed the street and
had never gone into that store, although it
would have been very convenient for me to deal
with them. So I started my "treatment" by picturing myself walking past the blind man, putting ten cents in his cup, and going into the
store. It made me feel a bit queasy at first, but I
relaxed myself more fully, and found that the
image did not bother me. I tried it out again the
next day and found that I could imagine it without feeling bad, even though I was not relaxing
at the time. So I decided to test it out immediately. I did exactly what I had imagined myself
doing—putting a dime into the blind man's cup
and walking into the store. I was amazed at how
simple it was. So then I tackled the next thing
on the list. I would say that it took me less than
a month to rid myself of all those phobias.*

If there are similar situations that make you
feel squeamish, or extremely tense, you might try

out the self-desensitization method. Remember the steps. (1) Try to relax as deeply as possible. Be sure that your entire body is comfortable before beginning the relaxation. It is best to sit down or to lie down so that each part of your body is fully supported and can comfortably switch off all tension. (2) Picture a relatively easy, not too disturbing, scene. If you can imagine it without feeling any anxiety or tension, proceed to a slightly more difficult image. If the image upsets you, switch it off and go back to the pure relaxation. After a few minutes of additional relaxation, picture the upsetting scene again and see if it bothers you less. Keep switching back and forth between the scene and the relaxation until you have weakened the feelings of anxiety or discomfort. (3) Be sure to finish every self-desensitization session on a relaxed and positive note. Do not stop when you feel tense or upset. Always go back to the relaxation so that you emerge with a sense of tranquillity.

By rehearsing these scenes over and over in a progressive fashion, always counterposing them with muscle relaxation, you can diminish the feelings of fear and anxiety step by step.

SOCIAL FEARS

Many people are afraid of things, situations, places, and events, but the most widespread fears and phobias concern our dealings with other people. These social fears are particularly significant and widespread. When a team of market researchers asked 3,000 U.S. inhabitants "What are you afraid of?" 41 percent answered, "Speaking before a group." The second most common fear, according to David Wallechinsky, Irving Wallace, and Amy Wallace in *The Book of Lists* is a fear of heights, followed by insects and bugs, financial problems, deep water, sickness, death, flying, loneliness, dogs, driving/riding in a car, darkness, elevators, and escalators. As Dr. Herbert Fensterheim, of Cornell University Medical College, points out, social fears are often camouflaged—many individuals have problems dealing with other people and fail to recognize that these difficulties stem from their own social fears. When you experience any type of social fear, people react to *your reaction,* and you thereby may automatically bring on the very thing you fear will happen. Thus, someone who fears rejection acts cold and aloof as a protective function and ends up getting rejected for being so unfriendly.

One of the most common social fears is to have others see that you are nervous. This is what often lies behind the number one fear—public speaking. To appear nervous, to shake or tremble in front of other people, to go blank and forget one's speech, and ultimately to pass out from sheer terror—that is the catalogue of horrors that many people impose on themselves when asked to address a group. Much of this is tied in with irrational ideas about being perfect, wanting to be infallible, and believing that any performance that shows up a personal shortcoming would render one foolish, stupid, inept, and incompetent.

My number one piece of advice for people who fear public speaking (and many people's jobs and livelihood depend on their willingness and ability to address groups) is to start one's speech by publicly declaring one's nervousness. "Good evening ladies and gentlemen. Before proceeding with my speech, I would first like to share a personal fact with you. Right now I am in a state of terror. Talking in front of groups always scares me to death. So if I drop dead you will understand exactly why!" This immediately undercuts the perfectionism and infallibility, and by dropping the phony facade that "nothing can scare *me*," one becomes human, the audience generally feels sympathetic, and the fears and tensions evaporate.

One of my patients said that he was too panicky before a group even to get as far as saying, "Good evening." In his case, he had to use self-desensitization beginning with the following image: "I am simply sitting on a stage with four other people in front of a large audience, but I do not have to be one of the speakers." He was quite calm as long as he did not have to speak to the audience, and so his self-desensitization proceeded with one word speeches and he slowly added words and sentences to his list. But some people, especially those who are *afraid of being looked at,* find the mere presence of other people extremely painful. Quite often, some obstinate phobias can be overcome by using the Step-Up Technique described in Chapter 2—especially when this is taken to the point of *mental flooding.*

For example, a young woman who had many

86

social phobias (fears of criticism, fears of rejection, fears of disapproval) did not respond to the usual desensitization techniques, but when she used the Step-Up Technique and flooded her mind with all types of rejections from others, her fears rapidly dissipated. ("I pictured everyone telling me that I am stupid, evil, nasty, hateful, and that they wanted nothing to do with me. I can't tell you why, but as I got further into this image, the whole thing seemed stupid and foolish to me. I tried to do it twice a day like you said, but by the third time I really couldn't picture it anymore. The image, and a lot of my fears that went into the image, just seemed to go away.") Unfortunately, there is no way of predicting in advance exactly which fear-reducing technique is most likely to succeed with a given individual. A certain amount of trial and error is unavoidable. That is why it is important for professional therapists to have a wide range of different methods in their treatment repertoire. I would hope that the reader of this book will acquire a wide range of effective imagery techniques for overcoming fears and for enhancing the joys of living.

OTHER IMAGERY METHODS THAT OVERCOME FEAR

Picturing Pleasant Scenes

The deliberate use of imagery can open many new possibilities. Consider the case of a man who consulted me about an urgent problem. He was flying from New York to Dallas the next day to visit his mother, who had become critically ill. "I suffer from claustrophobia," he explained, "and I've avoided traveling by plane. I develop a trapped and confined sensation and start feeling awful. I thought about driving down to Texas, but that would take far too long."

Some simple imagery tests showed that he was quite receptive and cooperative. For example, he could readily picture himself standing at a busy intersection, looking at a shop window, watching a piece of paper floating down a stream, seeing and hearing ocean waves rolling onto the shore. "If you use your powers of imagery," I explained, "you need not feel trapped or confined. In the plane, if you start developing claustrophobic sensations, close your eyes and picture yourself on a wide open beach. Look up at the blue sky, see some clouds floating high up, feel the warm sun on your back. And then imagine yourself high up on a mountainside overlooking a vast plain that stretches to the horizon. Feel the cool breeze on your face." We discussed and practiced visualizing several other non-claustrophobic scenes.

When he returned from Texas a few days later, he called to tell me that the imagery had worked perfectly. While flying down to Dallas he had begun to feel his usual panicky sensations, whereupon he immediately used the prescribed imagery. He did so three or four times and felt quite calm. On his return flight he did not need to use the imagery techniques and stated that he actually enjoyed the plane ride for the first time in his life.

The vividness of imagery becomes clearer with practice. Most people can learn how to project themselves into pleasure-arousing scenes. This simple skill can be used in many situations. I always employ it when visiting the dentist!

Coping Imagery

A direct method that I call *coping imagery* can also be used to overcome fears and phobias. You begin by picturing yourself in the feared situation. Study the unpleasant feelings and sensations that the image arouses. Next see yourself, in your mind's eye, coping with the situation. Imagine yourself as vividly as possible in the feared situation, but see yourself coping admirably, not feeling the least bit upset. If you can dwell on that image of positive coping in a phobic area of your life, there is an excellent chance that the actual situation will prove less troublesome. This is especially true if you rehearse this coping imagery each day for a couple of weeks.

In order to ensure that the coping imagery proves effective, ask yourself *exactly what you need to do* in order to see yourself coping with the fearful situation. Do you have to take some action? Do you have to define matters differently, such as convincing yourself that something terrible is merely inconvenient? For example, a young man with an extreme fear of rejection was terrified of asking attractive women for dates. While practicing coping imagery

89

he was to picture himself being turned down by a most attractive woman, but nonetheless to see himself handling the rejection without becoming upset.

He tried this out for a few days and then reported: "The only way I can visualize this without becoming upset is by first persuading myself that the main reason she said 'no' to me was because she had a jealous boyfriend whom she feared." I said, "That's fine, but now how about taking the risk of actually approaching women and asking them for dates while keeping that thought and image of the jealous boyfriend in your head?"

He took my suggestion, and went up to a woman he had long admired. "As I looked at her I went into my mental act. I told myself that due to her jealous boyfriend she will have to turn down anyone who asked her out. Once I had established this in my own mind, I simply asked her if she would like to have dinner with me and perhaps go to a movie. I was ready for her 'no thanks' and almost fell over when she said 'Thank you, I'd like to.' I did similar things with four other women and only struck out once—and it really didn't bother me because I 'knew' about the jealous boyfriend." This young man now enjoys an extremely active and rewarding social life.

People who acquire proficiency in the use of imagery have a marvelous built-in tool. I have seen many people who were once riddled with fears and phobias and who learned to cope with many difficult situations via mental imagery. As one former patient put it, "Whenever I'm in any sort of tight spot

I know that I can use positive imagery by thinking about pleasant experiences. I then switch off my fears and cope coolly and rationally with whatever comes down the pike.''

Many athletes have learned to quell their fears with imagery. I have treated several well-known boxers, swimmers, and golfers who developed specific fears before or during their matches. By learning to focus, when necessary, on constructive and relaxing imagery, they not only overcame their fears but also improved their athletic performance. When a championship jockey was injured during a horse race, he developed a phobia about riding horses. Two desensitization sessions, plus a week of coping imagery exercises at home, completely extinguished his fears. He went back to riding winners and did so without any trace of his former fears.

Imaginary Negative Reinforcement

Another useful imagery technique for overcoming phobias is what Dr. Joseph Cautela terms "covert negative reinforcement." I prefer the term "imaginary negative reinforcement." This is how it works.

Let's consider acrophobia (a morbid fear of heights). The person with acrophobia is first asked to imagine him or herself trapped in a burning building. Vivid imagery is presented of the flames shooting all over, the choking smoke, the terrifying heat, the collapsing walls, but just before the floor caves in, the person escapes onto a fireman's tall ladder, and profound relief is felt at being rescued from the burning building, even though one is hundreds of feet up from the ground before climbing down the ladder. The mechanism behind this technique is simple: *When you repeatedly picture something fearful saving you from an even greater terror, the original fear often diminishes in strength and takes on a different meaning.*

I used imaginary negative reinforcement with a young woman who suffered from claustrophobia. She did not respond to the more usual fear-control techniques, so I decided to try out the imaginary negative reinforcement method. We created a vivid story in which she was being followed by a dangerous-looking man who turned out to be a member of a gang that was out to kill her. (To make the story credible, we had to introduce the theme of a case of mistaken identity.) She had a vivid imagination and was able to experience high levels of anxiety when picturing various scenes. In one of them, she was in the basement garage and the men were searching for her. She was with a friend, and the only means of escape would be for the friend to lock her in the trunk of a car. We agreed that the assassins would look in each car but that they would not think of breaking open the trunk. She then pictured herself shut up in the trunk of the car where it soon became hot and stuffy. (Ordinarily, this image would have generated extreme anxiety but under these special circumstances, she felt safe rather than panicky.) After some time the men gave up their hunt and left. Knowing that she was safe led her to feel profound relief from anxiety, despite the image of still being locked in the trunk of the car, and waiting for her friend to release her.

Imaginary negative reinforcement overcame her claustrophobia in four sessions. When entering real-life situations that tended to bring on attacks of tension and anxiety (such as crowded rooms, the middle aisle of a theater, or wedged in the corner at a busy restaurant) she would imagine that a greater danger awaited her if she left the scene. "Immediately, I would begin to calm down. Now it doesn't bother me at all."

If you have any fears, phobias, or undue sensitivities, one or more of the methods outlined in this chapter should prove effective in ridding you of these unpleasant reactions. Whether you elect systematic desensitization from a professional therapist, or decide to try a regimen of self-desensitization (perhaps using "pleasant imagery," or "coping imagery," or "imaginary negative reinforcement" to augment the process) you are likely to overcome these "hangups" if you apply imagery techniques in a diligent way.

Fears and phobias seldom disappear on their own. There is a psychological dictum that says: "You cannot extinguish a response in the absence of a stimulus." This means that if you avoid the stimuli that arouse anxiety in you, they will always remain capable of creating emotional upsets. When you face these stimuli repeatedly and weaken them systematically, you become liberated from the constraints of fear. And in order to achieve this end, most people do not need to face the "actual" stimuli; with vivid imagery, the necessary stimuli are dealt with phenomenologically, and the associated fears tend to wither away. This chapter has provided several specific imagery procedures that can allow your non-phobic reactions to win out over your phobic responses. These techniques have helped thousands of people. As further chapters will show, apart from overcoming phobias, imagery has much to offer everyone who is interested in self-improvement and self-fulfillment. But first, those of you who have children with fears and phobias might like to know what to do for your youngsters.

CHAPTER 6

Overcoming Children's Fears and Anxieties with Imagery Techniques

Most children have vivid and active imaginations. A child's mind is often filled with lively and frightening imagery—ghosts, goblins, phantoms, and monsters. Small wonder that many children have fears and phobias.

As outlined in the previous chapter, in order to understand the basis of a phobia one must appreciate the subjective imagery that causes it. A child who is afraid of the dark is obviously not fearful of darkness as such. The fears revolve around images of *what* may lurk in the darkness. His or her imagery may involve attacks from demons, vampires, spooks, and many other apparitions. The basis of these fears often stems from cruel nurses, misguided parents, unfortunate fairy tales, and ill-conceived television programs.

The fearful or phobic child suffers extensively.

Childhood is a period of life when one is objectively at the mercy of others. One is smaller, weaker, less knowledgeable, and dependent upon adults. To add specific irrational fears to the widespread uncertainties of childhood compounds the miseries. The child who is reared in an atmosphere of warmth, kindness, and understanding is most fortunate. While many people assert that childhood is the happiest time of life, it is easy to dispel certain glorified and romantic ideals by taking imaginary trips back in time and seeing what it felt like really to be a young child. The phobic child is often teased and ridiculed by his or her peers. Adults who know no better try to "help" the child by using mockery. You do not have to be a trained therapist to apply the imagery methods outlined in this chapter for overcoming children's fears and phobias. Imagery techniques may be employed not only for conquering or surmounting specific phobias; they also have a useful preventive function, as we shall see.

I first made extensive use of imagery with children in 1961. At the time I was treating a number of phobic children with the help of Dr. Arnold Abramovitz, now at the University of Cape Town, South Africa. We found that the desensitization methods based on imagery and relaxation (outlined in Chapter 5) proved successful with several phobic children, but many of them, especially the younger children, did not cooperate with the relaxation instructions. As we saw more and more cases, we found that whereas most adults responded exceedingly well to relaxation training, it became both time-consuming

96

and difficult, or impossible, to achieve relaxation with many children. We then explored the possibility of using positive images in place of relaxation.

Since we were dealing primarily with children's phobias, we were interested in developing images that could erase the child's phobic imagery. Thus, the kinds of imagery we investigated were those that aroused *anti-anxiety* emotions, such as pride, joy, mirth, affection, self-assertion, and the like. We called these images, which can arouse pleasant emotions and non-anxious feelings, *emotive imagery*.

APPLYING EMOTIVE IMAGERY

One of the first cases to be treated by emotive imagery was a 14-year-old boy who suffered from an intense fear of dogs. He was sadly unresponsive to attempts at training in relaxation. In his desire to please, he would state that he was perfectly relaxed, but he betrayed himself by intense fidgetiness. Consequently, we decided to use emotive imagery. He was carefully questioned about his likes, dislikes, ambitions, and passions. It seemed that he had a burning desire to own and race an Alfa Romeo sports car. As soon as he was old enough, he wanted to race at the Indianapolis "500" event. We decided to employ this image in an attempt to overcome his phobia.

The boy was so terrified of dogs (his fears had started when he was about eleven years old) that he would take two buses on a roundabout route to school rather than risk exposure to dogs on a direct

300-yard walk. Emotive imagery was induced as follows: "Close your eyes. I want you to imagine, clearly and vividly, that your wish has come true. The Alfa Romeo is now in your possession. It is your car. It is standing on the street outside your block. You are looking at it now. Notice the beautiful sleek lines. You decide to go for a drive with some friends of yours. You sit down at the wheel, and you feel a thrill of pride as you realize that you own this magnificent machine. You start up the engine and you listen to the wonderful roar. You let the clutch out and the car streaks off. . . . You are out in a clear open road now; the car is performing perfectly; the speedometer is climbing into the nineties; you have a wonderful feeling of being in perfect control; you look at the trees whizzing by you and you see a little dog standing next to one of them—if you feel any anxiety just raise your finger."

If he raised his finger, we would go back to the imagery and create even greater positive feelings before reintroducing the feared stimulus. Since he did not signal anxiety, the image was continued and this time he whizzed by a much larger dog. Next, he drove past one which was barking. At no time did he feel anxious. The emotive image was far too enjoyable. Even the following item did not generate any anxiety: "You stop at a café in a little town and dozens of people crowd round to look enviously at this magnificent car and its lucky owner; you swell with pride; and at this moment a large dog comes up and sniffs at your heels."

After three sessions of emotive imagery, the

boy reported a marked improvement in his reaction to dogs. He was then asked to see whether he could stop running away from dogs in real life. This posed no problem. A year later we contacted the boy and his family. They all said that there was no longer any trace of his former phobia.

Apart from ridding children of their specific phobias, emotive imagery seems to have diverse and positive effects on many facets of the child's personality. Children who have overcome phobic reactions often find that their schoolwork improves, and that many more subtle manifestations of insecurity disappear. This is not surprising, because a phobia can lower a child's general morale and erode his or her self-confidence.

BATMAN AND ROBIN OVERCOME A CHILD'S SCHOOL PHOBIA

In administering emotive imagery with children, one discusses with the child his or her hero-images, usually derived from television, movies, fiction stories, or the child's own imagination. One carefully looks for the child's wishes about his or her *alter ego*. With a great many children in recent years, Batman and Robin have featured prominently.

For instance, the parents of a 9-year-old boy were most perturbed at their child's reluctance to go to school. His problems had developed gradually. A rather disturbed and sadistic teacher had unfairly reprimanded the child several times. Although the teacher had left the school, the child nevertheless became fearful before leaving for school in the mornings. Within a few weeks, each morning before school, the boy would complain that he was ill. He threw up on two separate occasions, and was obviously extremely distressed.

I conducted a thorough diagnostic interview with the parents and tested the boy with several scholastic and personality measures. These interviews and tests were administred to find out (a) whether possible problems between the parents were upsetting the child; (b) whether the mother or the father had vested interests in keeping the child at home (some children develop "school phobias" because their *parents* are over-anxious about their welfare when away from home!); (c) whether the child was scholastically deficient, which might account for his anxieties; and (d) whether the child was so dependent on his mother that he suffered not from "school phobia" but from "separation anxiety" (some so-called school phobic children are not so much afraid of the school situation as they are of leaving their mother's side).

The young boy showed up as very intelligent on the tests, and I could find nothing in his personality or in his home life that led me to suspect anything other than "school phobia." The child's imagery indicated that his fears arose from pictures of receiving additional punishment at the hands of nasty teachers. Although the school principal and all the boy's current teachers were most kind and understanding, his negative images persisted.

The boy's favorite heroes were Batman and

100

Robin, the comicbook and television super-sleuths who fight crime while disguised in colorful costumes. I applied emotive imagery by telling the boy the following story:

"Imagine that Batman and Robin have asked you to assist them in catching a criminal. They lend you a special wrist radio so that they can contact you whenever necessary. Nobody must know the secret, that you are actually helping Batman and Robin to solve a crime right in your own school. Batman says to you 'Peter, I have placed a secret message in your school locker. When you get to school tomorrow morning, go to your locker as soon as possible and read the message. Then destroy it!' Of course you don't want to tell Batman and Robin about your fears, so you go to school the next morning and head straight for your locker. Picture yourself going to school. As you ride toward the school in the bus, you are wondering what the message will say. You get into the school yard, get out of the bus, and you walk slowly to your locker. You don't want to rush there because you don't want to make anyone suspicious."

At this point in the story I asked the boy to tell me in great detail what was happening. He described the school building, the hallway along which he was walking, the other children, opening his locker. The reason for this was to enable the child to see himself back at school without feeling anxious. In place of the fear was the curiosity, the fun, the excitement, and the drama—what would the message say? I continued the emotive imagery.

"You open your locker and there you see a slip of green paper. It has the emblem of a bat on it and you know who the sender is. You slip it into your pocket, and some of your friends come up and talk to you. As soon as you manage to do so without being seen, you read the message from Batman and Robin. It says: 'We will signal you on your wrist radio during your first recess. Over and out!' You go to class, the teacher gives you some work to do. You are sitting at your desk working. You wonder what Batman and Robin will want you to do next. You carry on with your work. The nasty teacher who left the school comes back into the classroom. You look at him, but you can't let that bother you. Bigger things are at stake. What will Batman and Robin ask you to do?"

I focused on the "nasty teacher" for quite a while in the emotive imagery so as to change the boy's emotions from fear to relative indifference. When one knows the cause of a child's fear, it is often helpful to change the imagery surrounding that fear. Thus, the "nasty teacher" who had supposedly engendered the boy's subsequent phobic reactions was now back in the picture, except that the images and the circumstances surrounding him were now quite different. Of course, when Batman and Robin finally contacted him on the wrist radio they stressed that the "nasty teacher" was in fact the person they were after. Peter was asked to keep the "nasty teacher" under surveillance. I had Robin tell the boy, "That man may get to be very nasty, but just ignore him."

102

At this point, Peter, verbalizing his own pent-up aggressions, insisted on finishing the story himself. He told me how he would help Batman and Robin to lure the nasty teacher into a trap so that they could capture him and remove him to the nearest jail. At the end of the session I asked Peter if he would try out his own Batman and Robin fantasy in school the next day. (Notice that I did not ask him *if* he would go to school the next day. What we call the "demand characteristics" of the situation placed the emphasis upon how well Peter would carry out his own fantasy projection *in school*.) Unfortunately, not many cases are that easily resolved, but after that one emotive imagery session, Peter went back to school and has had no additional problems.

Some people may be concerned that the emotive imagery procedure plays tricks with a child's mind and encourages the child to daydream and to dwell on fantasy rather than on reality. I have treated many dozens of children with emotive imagery and have found no negative side effects. I have never come across a child who failed to differentiate fantasy from reality in the emotive imagery. And if children and adults sometimes employ fantasy in order to help them to cope with harsh reality, what harm can follow?

THE PREVENTIVE IMPLICATIONS OF POSITIVE IMAGERY

Instead of filling children's minds with dreadful monsters and bogeymen, or in place of meaningless fairy tales, what would occur if they were told numerous stories involving reality-based *coping imagery?* For example, an imaginative parent in telling stories to a child could instill basic psychological realities. One could weave a theme around the important fact that it is quite permissible to make mistakes instead of trying to be perfect. Here, the hero would learn the importance of profiting from one's own errors, and imaginative stories could emphasize the point that learning through mistakes is one of the best forms of personal education. Being taught that it is not necessary to be correct all the time and realizing that everyone is fallible are psychological truths well worth cultivating right from the start. And through imaginative stories, children can be shown that most things in life are not "either/or," "right/wrong," "good/bad."

While consulting at a nursery school, I remember sitting down with a group of 4- and 5-year-old children and, through imagery stories, showing them how to cope with difficult situations. For example, I told the story of a make-believe little girl whom we called Pamela. While in a large shopping center with her mother, Pamela discovered that she was lost. She didn't cry or become afraid. Pamela went into one of the stores and told the salesperson standing behind the counter that she was lost. The children and I discussed other options that were open to Pamela; what she would do if she could not find a salesperson behind a counter, the best thing to do if lost at a supermarket, or at a parade, or if lost in one's own neighborhood. The image of little Pamela solving all these practical puzzles kept the children alert, interested, and responsive. It provided them with many practical and reassuring steps that can be taken in many situations to avoid unnecessary panic and fear.

One of my friends mentioned that her 4-year-old daughter was developing a fear of doctors. The child had received some injections and, shortly thereafter, her fears became evident. I advised the mother to use emotive imagery. Each night she told her daughter a bedtime story involving benevolent doctors who were particularly kind to little girls and took away their pains and illnesses. About four months after this nightly routine had started, the child developed a strep throat and required medical attention. She showed no fear of the doctor, was a most cooperative patient, and remarked how the physician had made her feel better "like the story said." In this way a possible phobia was nipped in the bud.

THE BASIC STEPS IN APPLYING EMOTIVE IMAGERY WITH CHILDREN

1. Try to establish, by means of sympathetic discussion, the range, intensity, and circumstances of the child's fears. What produces the fear? When is it a little better, and when is it at its worst? How does the child cope with it? Attempt to draw up a graduated list from the least feared to the most feared situations.

2. Try to establish the nature of the child's hero-images—usually derived from TV, movies, radio, fiction, or the child's own imagination. You are searching for some powerful and reassuring companion to weave into stories involving the child's fears.

3. As described in this chapter, you then ask the child to close his or her eyes, and you describe an imaginary sequence of events that is close enough to the child's everyday life to be credible. Within the story, you introduce the child's favorite hero or *alter ego*. (You might re-read the way in which Batman and Robin were presented to Peter on pages 101–102.)

4. Each time the fear-arousing scenes are presented (starting with the least fearful events) introduce the hero-images as a natural part of the narrative. Immediately afterwards, ask the child if he/she felt afraid, unhappy, or uncomfortable. If so, introduce more and more pleasant scenes involving the child and the hero-images, and do not move to a more difficult item until the child no longer feels any tension or fear when picturing the less fearful scenes. Another brief case study might further clarify the method.

THIS IS A CASE FOR SUPERMAN!

A 10-year-old boy was terrified of the dark. He became acutely anxious when his parents went visiting at night, and even when they were at his side, he refused to enter any darkened room. He made constant use of a night light next to his bed. The boy was not anxious during the day, but he invariably became tense and afraid toward sunset.

His fears seemed to have originated about a year previously when he saw a frightening film and shortly thereafter was warned by his grandmother to keep away from all doors and windows at night as burglars and kidnappers were on the prowl. The boy's parents had taken him to a psychiatrist for several months, but his terror of the dark remained unchanged. In addition to his fear of the dark, the child was troubled by nightmares, and his school-work was deteriorating. The use of emotive imagery eliminated his fears in three sessions.

The boy was extremely fond of "Superman" stories and we therefore used "The Man of Steel" as his hero-image. The child was to imagine that Superman had asked him to be one of his new "secret agents." He was told: "Now I want you to close your eyes and imagine that you are sitting in the dining room with your mother and father. It is night time. Suddenly you receive a signal on the wrist radio that Superman has given you. You quickly run into the living room because your mission must be kept secret. There is only a little light coming into the living room from the hallway. Now pretend that you are all alone in the living room waiting for Superman to visit you. Think about this very clearly . . ."

The boy would then report on his feelings. When any scene aroused his anxiety, it would be altered slightly so as to prove less threatening. For example, this scene evoked some initial anxiety: "You are all alone in your bedroom, it is pitch black, and you are looking out of the window to see if Superman is coming." This instruction was added: "Let your eyes grow accustomed to the dark and you will notice that you can see pretty well—that as you relax and wait for your eyes to adjust, you can see quite clearly, and things seem lighter."

At the end of the third session (he was seen for an hour once a week) the child was able to picture himself alone in the bathroom with all the lights turned off, awaiting a communication from Superman. In addition to overcoming his fear of the dark, this method seemed to have a positive effect on the boy's daily life. His schoolwork improved and many other manifestations of fear and insecurity were no longer apparent. About a year later, his mother commented that he had become "a completely different child" in a very positive way.

Emotive imagery has been a most useful method for overcoming children's phobias. Several years ago, an 11-year-old girl whom I had treated referred to me as "the man who takes away fear." I have used emotive imagery to good effect with my patients, with several of my friends' children, and with my own children. The dreads and terrors of a phobic child are extremely painful. It is so easy for a child to feel all alone, vulnerable, confused, and very frightened. Any method that can assuage these negative emotions is well worth cultivating.

PART III

Using Imagery to Overcome Problems

CHAPTER 7

How Imagery Can Help You Break Habits

Thus far, we have been emphasizing the acquisition of *positive imagery* for overcoming fears, phobias, and related problems. Now let us explore the role of negative imagery for the reduction or eradication of a different set of problems.

I first employed negative imagery in 1957 when treating a 36-year-old architect who suffered from compulsions to "check and re-check everything." This compulsive checking proved to be a hindrance in his job, so much so that, despite being a qualified architect, he was working as a draftsman. "I check the scales again and again and even though I know that the detail is correctly mapped, I go over the same figure about ten times before I do the next one. Sometimes it nearly drives me mad, but I have to go on and on."

The full details of this case were published in 1958, but for our purposes I would like to underscore the negative imagery technique that I employed to overcome his compulsions. He was hypnotized and given more or less the following instructions: "You feel calm and relaxed, deeply relaxed and peaceful. Now I want you to imagine yourself at work. You still feel calm and relaxed. Now imagine yourself drawing a plan and checking it as you go along. You're quite relaxed. You check it once. Everything is correct. You make sure and go over it again. You are still calm and relaxed. You begin to check it a third time, but now suddenly you feel anxious. You feel uneasy and tense. Rapidly the tension mounts. (He was writhing and breathing very heavily at this stage.) You leave the plan. You do not check it again. Now you start a new drawing. Picture the new situation. As soon as you start the new activity you are once again calm and relaxed. You feel calm and peaceful. . . . When I count up to five you will open your eyes."

The rationale is quite straightforward. It is legitimate to check a design once or twice, but anything beyond that seems unnecessary and neurotic. Consequently, positive imagery was employed while he was behaving adaptively, but as soon as he started behaving maladaptively—by starting to check the drawing for the third time—negative imagery was introduced to make him feel tense and uneasy. If he came to associate excessive checking with "mounting tension, anxiety, general uneasiness, and other unpleasant sensations," he might stop this self-defeating habit and start behaving more appropriately. This would be even more likely if he associated pleasant imagery and wholesome feelings with appropriate behavior. Hence the statement "as soon as you start the new activity you are once again calm and relaxed."

He received ten negative imagery sessions, each lasting for about thirty minutes, over a five-week period. He then reported that his compulsions no longer troubled him in the work situation. "I'm turning out five times more work than before. . . . Sometimes I still tend to fuss over things more than I ought to, but that doesn't worry me."

Although hypnosis was employed in the abovementioned case, it is by no means a necessary part of the treatment. In fact, I stopped using hypnosis with the negative imagery technique because it wastes time. However, relaxation does help the imagery, especially if the person relaxes before picturing the scenes. For example, soon after I treated the compulsive architect I was consulted by a man who wanted to drink less alcohol. He was not an "alcoholic" but frequently had too much to drink at parties and would end up regretting it. We agreed that he was not to exceed three drinks. Since he was exclusively a whiskey drinker, we defined a drink as 1½ ounces of whiskey. He was a large and heavily built man, well over 200 pounds, and we estimated that he could handle up to 4½ ounces of spirits during the course of an evening. After relaxing him, I asked him to imagine having one drink, then another, and later on a third shot of whiskey. However, the moment he exceeded this limit he would begin to feel nauseous. As soon as he would bring that fourth drink to his lips he was to picture a variety of unpleasant scenes. Of course, this technique requires the client's full cooperation, but for people who genuinely wish to increase their "self-control," negative imagery introduced at judicious moments can be most effective. Since the mid-1960s many clinicians have reported that negative imagery techniques are helpful in extinguishing unwanted behaviors and thereby allowing desired behaviors to emerge.

Dr. Joseph R. Cautela of Boston College has carried out extensive work on negative imagery in treating a variety of problems such as smoking, stealing, obesity, and sexual deviations (e.g., exhibitionism, voyeurism, child molesting). When treating difficult cases such as addicts or alcoholics, it is necessary to make the negative imagery distinctly aversive. Thus, in great and deliberately nauseating detail Dr. Cautela will have an alcoholic imagining himself having a drink and immediately feeling queasy in the pit of his stomach. The first swallow of the drink is regurgitated together with bitter tasting particles of food that create a choking feeling as he tries to swallow. The discomfort increases as he feels sicker and sicker with tears and mucus and saliva drooling down his face into his drink. Then with a sickly loud heave, he pictures himself vomiting all over himself, onto the floor and into his drink—ugly smelling yellow bits of green slimy vomit. He continues to retch and gets sick over and over again with more and more vomit covering everything. The odor is dreadful, and makes him want to vomit even more. He takes another sip of his drink which is full of floating mucus, food particles, and smelly vomit. He tries to vomit again but can only have dry heaves. So he throws away the drink, turns away from all the other bottles of alcohol, gets far away from all booze into clean fresh air and begins to feel really great. Then he dives into a cool bubbling brook (or steps into a gentle warm shower, as the case may be), and emerges completely clean and wholesome.

It is a rare person who can read the foregoing paragraph, picture the scene, and not feel the least tinge of nausea him- or herself. It certainly demonstrates the power of negative imagery! In one treatment session, an alcoholic patient might work through about twenty different aversive scenes and then be encouraged to practice similar scenes between sessions. The therapist may prepare cassette recordings of nauseating scenes for the patient to use at home. There are several reports in the professional literature attesting to the efficacy of these techniques, even with chronic alcoholics.

The techniques of negative imagery for reducing or eliminating undesirable habits and behaviors are all very similar. If the aim is to cut down on cigarette smoking, the images involve vomiting upon inhaling the smoke, smoking cigarettes dipped in vomit, focusing on images pertaining to lung cancer, lip cancer, throat cancer. When treating obesity, or simply adhering to a diet, the images involve nauseating and dreadful consequences upon eating forbidden foodstuffs. These negative images can certainly promote self-control or so-called willpower. In fact, it is my impression that people who successfully manage to exercise self-control have ready-made or built-in aversive images at their disposal. One woman who lost nearly fifty pounds in eight months told me how she had adhered to her diet. She took a pound of fat and placed it in a transparent polyethylene bag. The fat in the bag looked repulsive. She showed it to all her friends. "That's what a pound of fat looks like," she told them. Whenever she was tempted to stray from her diet, she would immediately picture the pound of fat. For every pound that she wanted to lose, she vividly imagined a polyethylene bag of fat stuck to her body.

Another woman solved the problem of maintaining an 83-pound weight loss that she had gradually achieved over a ten-month period. "All my life I have had the yo-yo syndrome," she explained. "I once lost fifty pounds and then promptly gained it all back plus more, and then I lost sixty pounds and gained it back, and so on." Indeed, as research has shown, nearly everyone can lose weight; the biggest problem is how to keep off the lost weight. Her solution was simple. She had two photographs in her wallet. One was a "before" picture of herself weighing 203 pounds, and the other was a more recent photograph where she weighed 120 pounds. "Whenever I feel a strong urge or temptation to eat more than I should, I immediately set the two photos side by side. I look at them and study them. Then I close my eyes and imagine myself weighing over 200

116

pounds. Immediately the urge to eat goes out the window!''

Before applying negative imagery, it is important to achieve a mood and feeling-tone that is receptive to the most vivid imagery. Most people find that their imagery is best stimulated if preceded by some deliberate muscle relaxation while stretched out on a comfortable bed, or couch, or mat.

THE DOCTOR'S FETISH

Relatively few practitioners are familiar with the technique of negative imagery. Several years ago, I was consulted by a family doctor who had seen two psychiatrists and several psychologists in search of a cure for what he called a ''sexual fetish.'' The doctor had an obsession about female genitalia. ''I have an overriding urge and desire to look at and touch the vaginas of every woman I examine.'' There was no problem when he was conducting a necessary pelvic examination, but women with headaches or sore throats were inclined to be puzzled when asked to undress! He feared that they would report him to the American Medical Association.

His previous therapy had all consisted of explorations into his past to try to explain his obsession. He was asked about his mother's behavior, his relationship to his older sister, his psycho-sexual history, and so forth. His various psychiatric treatments extended over six years, but his obsession re-

117

mained unchanged, and he continued taking extreme risks with the women he examined in his day-to-day work. By the time he had consulted me, he had been reported to an ethics committee by at least one of his patients, and he suspected that word had leaked out about his behavior.

I explained the rationale and procedure of negative imagery to him. It was clear that when carrying out unnecessary vaginal examinations on female patients, he concentrated solely on the sexual arousal it engendered in him. At those times he gave no thought to the risks and negative consequences. Although he always carried out his examinations with a female nurse present (who knew about and indulged his obsession) many women expressed their indignation, while others rightly refused to be examined. At times his obsession was so strong that he unwisely argued with the women who did not comply. Again, his attention was riveted on his own sexual arousal, without any thought of the consequences. In our first session of negative imagery I therefore concentrated on all the possible negative consequences.

After relaxing him, I had him imagine a typical sequence. He was consulted by a female patient who complained of earache. After examining her ears, nose, and throat, he asked her to undress. She obliged. He called in his nurse, examined the patient's breasts and then looked at her genitals. However, she was a police decoy sent by the Ethics Board, and the moment he touched her vagina his office was overrun by uniformed policewomen. He was handed a summons and escorted to the nearest police station. He was charged with unprofessional conduct and various other illegal acts, was thrown in jail, released on bail, and made headline news in the local paper as a "pervert" and "sexual maniac." As the negative image continued, he had to endure shame and extensive disgrace.

I made the negative images extremely vivid. The narration, like a never-ending nightmare, was presented continuously for almost one hour at the end of which the doctor looked pale and shaky, he was perspiring and complained of nausea and dizziness. "Remember those feelings and remember the negative imagery," I said. And then I gave him the key instruction: "The very next woman you decide to examine unnecessarily may turn out to be a police decoy."

He came to see me again after two weeks. "It's been working pretty well," he said, "I haven't been tempted to do anything silly, but I think the effects are beginning to wear off." I explained to him that negative imagery had to be used by him in an active manner so as to keep its effects alive. The moment any temptation was felt, instead of giving in he was to stop for a moment, picture the police decoy scenario, and then he would find it much easier to resist the temptation. We then repeated the negative image, only this time I made it even more unpleasant by having him picture his parents' reaction, as well as the hurt and puzzled look on his younger brother's face. From then on, the doctor was able to "resist temptation." His "fetish" grew weaker over the years, but whenever he felt the slightest urge to transgress his professional responsibilities, he would conjure up a negative image to keep himself in check.

THE SUICIDAL SENIOR

It may prove illuminating to outline how negative imagery was applied to a 17-year-old suicidal girl, and how it completely altered her mental outlook. The distraught parents consulted me about their daughter, a high school senior with a long history of psychiatric disturbance. Despite the assistance of several therapists, she had tried killing herself three times over a period of six months—twice by taking an overdose of pills, and once by slashing her wrists. She was close to death on the last attempt and kept insisting that she would "get it right" the next time.

Various professionals had labeled the girl "manic depressive," or "schizophrenic," or "psychopathic," or "hysterical," but these diagnoses failed to provide a coherent explanation of her self-destructive tendencies. Her anger, anxiety, confusion, and guilt were all clearly evident, but her basic motives became clear only when I applied the following imagery:

"I want you to imagine that you are dead. You have killed yourself, and now you are an invisible spirit looking at the events after your funeral. What do you see?" Up to this point, she answered every question with, "I don't know," but this time she described a scene in which her parents, especially her mother, would be broken-hearted. She went on to describe how the entire family, including aunts, uncles, cousins, and her two sisters would be sorry for mistreating her. They would suffer continuous pangs of guilt and remorse, and as time dragged on, they would all wish to be dead themselves.

This revengeful image gave her feelings of great personal satisfaction. She was extremely immature and had developed highly irrational rage and resentment toward her family. By committing suicide, she imagined that she would be getting back at them and that they would suffer lifelong regrets. "That's not how it will work!" I insisted. Then I vividly described a scene in which she was dead, buried, and rotting in a dank grave while each member of her family recovered from their initial grief, enjoyed life, sunshine, fresh air, and partook of fun and laughter while the worms were devouring her decaying remains. I stressed how, with the passage of time, they would think of her and remember her less and less until she became a faint and almost nonexistent memory. I emphasized how, by the time her skeleton was crumbling to dust, she would be long-forgotten while they would all be having fun that she would have missed out all these years.

She seemed taken aback. "You're probably right," she conceded. Our therapy then turned to the way in which she could learn to live her own life and to pursue her own happiness—with or without the love and the approval of her family. In this case, the negative imagery also opened up therapeutic channels of communication and enabled me to establish rapport.

People who take the time to sharpen their negative imagery will possess a useful tool for checking their undesirable habits and thereby gain self-control. Studies at Stanford University have demonstrated that even young children can employ imagery to help them "resist temptation." In one experiment the children were sitting at a table with a plate of delicious marshmallows in front of them. They were told to see how long they could "delay gratification" by not eating a single marshmallow. When the experimenter, Dr. Walter Mischel, instructed some children to *transform the real objects in front of them into color pictures in their head, to pretend that the tasty marshmallows were actually dry cotton balls,* the children were able to resist temptation for long periods of time. The latter example is not one of aversive imagery but is simply an example of the powers of *negative imagery*. Let us now discuss the way in which negative imagery can be combined with positive rewards.

COMBINING NEGATIVE IMAGERY WITH POSITIVE REWARDS

A combination of negative imagery with positive rewards proved particularly useful to a young married woman who had good reason to resent her mother-in-law, and to anticipate her visits with some trepidation. The young woman would invariably end up fighting with her husband before, during, and after a visit from her mother-in-law. The wife's tension and irritability would increase prior to the visit, and she would usually try to persuade her husband to cancel his mother's impending arrival. He would point out that his mother was a kind, if misguided woman, who often made tactless remarks and who inadvertently antagonized other people without meaning to do so. "She means well," the husband would explain, "but she's rather silly and inappropriate. Can't you be big enough to overlook her annoying faults?" The wife would feel petty, stupid, and intolerant, and then she would resolve to be "big about it." But the old woman would soon break through these good resolutions by volunteering gratuitous advice and a barrage of criticism, to which the young woman would feel compelled to defend herself, and then she would end up engaging in futile rhetoric with her mother-in-law.

Since these visits amounted to less than a total of six hours every three or four months, it seemed that the wife would be better off avoiding any discourse with her mother-in-law. Nor was there much point to altering her husband's exaggerated attachment for his mother. She felt that if she could control her temper and simply humor the old lady by agreeing with her, everyone would derive much benefit. Accordingly, I used the following imagery technique. "Relax. Let your muscles go loose. Feel heavy and calm. . . . Now I want you to picture your mother-in-law saying some particularly outrageous things to you. She is implying that you are a rotten person, that her son deserves far better, that you are dishonest, inefficient, and quite worthless as a wife, as a daughter-in-law, and as a human being. . . . Now see yourself smiling through all this; see yourself ignoring it." At this point she opened her eyes and said, "I can't do it. Even the image makes me so mad that I would like to kick her." Consequently, I asked her to imagine that she was under surveillance and that she would face a firing squad if she as much as ventured an opinion. But if she endured her mother-in-law's harangue without incident, a reward would be forthcoming. We decided that the reward would be a dinner treat by her husband at a restaurant of her choosing.

The husband agreed to the plan. If his wife remained entirely pleasant and avoided any contentious interchange, he would immediately follow up his mother's visit by taking his wife out for dinner. The result was eminently positive. The wife was able to deal with her mother-in-law regardless of the old woman's barbs. Several months later, the wife told me that she had stopped using the imagery technique on the assumption that the anticipated treat of dining out with her husband would be enough to deter her from quarreling with her mother-in-law. However, this proved insufficient. When she failed to practice the "firing squad" imagery, she invariably fought with her mother-in-law; ended up feeling weak, guilty, and immature, forfeited a pleasant dinner, argued with her husband, and suffered considerable misery. But the combined negative image and the positive reward were sufficient to contain her anger, and resulted in the development of an appropriate and fitting indifference to her mother-in-law's innuendos.

WILLPOWER AND IMAGERY

Some people seem to have much greater "willpower" than others. They can refuse tempting foods, quit smoking, and generally avoid indulging in various excesses or bad habits. I believe that these so-called strong-willed people are able to break bad habits, not because of some "inner strength" per se, but because they have a well-defined image of the negative consequences. If you needed to lose weight and found yourself confronted by an array of delicious candy, cakes, cookies, pies, ice creams and other forbidden foodstuffs, would you eat any of them if you had a vivid picture of your heart and arteries getting clogged up with cholesterol, of the added sugar in your body causing oozing globules of fat to accumulate? Not likely! What happens with the "weak-willed" person is that he or she does *not* form an image of the negative consequences, but focuses instead on the pleasures of eating, sucking, tasting, smelling, and digesting the delectable foods. The various examples outlined in this chapter should provide you with a direct means toward the attainment of powerful "willpower."

The basic lesson to be learned is that whenever you find yourself tempted to gravitate toward something that you know will prove detrimental, stop for a few moments and construct a negative image of the unfortunate consequences. Do not concentrate on the positives ("That chocolate will taste so good, it will melt in my mouth and slide gently and warmly down my throat!") but dwell on the negatives ("That chocolate is poison! It will do damage! It will clog up my arteries! It could lead to a heart attack! It will add fat to my body—ugly globules of fat!"). If the one or two negative images prove insufficient and you still find yourself craving the chocolate, you might introduce a pure aversive image. ("I will pretend that the chocolate has been dipped in vomit and is covered with arsenic!" "It will stick in my throat and I will gag and choke on it if I eat it!") These procedures should assist you in moving away from the temptation, and when you manage to beat the urge, you might give yourself a reward. ("Because I ate no candy and had no desserts all week, I am going to buy myself a new record album.")

In this chapter, we have described several specific images that can help you achieve self-control in a variety of situations. The next chapter will show you how to control that most widespread negative emotion of them all—sadness or unhappiness. Indeed, the imagery modality is extremely versatile and, as we shall see in succeeding chapters, it can be used to excellent advantage in a wide variety of personal and interpersonal situations.

CHAPTER 8

The Role of Imagery in Overcoming Sadness and Despondency

Many people suffer a condition where all joy goes out of life and a heavy gloom pervades their existence and hangs like a dark pall over every facet of their being. They lose their zest for living, and the fun goes out of everything. These people are not only "sad"; they are *depressed*. Often they have a characteristic pattern, wherein they feel at their worst in the mornings (especially the early morning hours before dawn), but as the day wears on and as evening approaches their mood may lighten slightly. They suffer from insomnia, especially intermittent waking throughout the night, and after their light and fitful sleep they stay awake in the early morning hours, unable to get back to sleep again. Especially at this time their morbid thoughts race on and on into ever deepening pools of misery. They have little appetite, they tend to lose weight, and their desire for sex usually dries up. They are often consumed by negative feelings of personal unworthiness and despair.

Several physiological conditions can give rise to depression. Among the best known are post-influenza depressions, post-partum depressions (after childbirth), and hypothyroidism (underactive thyroid gland). Many experts agree that depression is the result of some biochemical disturbance. The reason I am dwelling on "depression" is because I want to separate this *medical disorder that usually calls for anti-depressant medication and other psychiatric interventions* from the day-to-day "downs" we all experience from time to time, from the occasional "blues," and the disappointments and frustrations that can nullify our *joie de vivre*. The imagery techniques described in this chapter are aimed at eliminating these latter types of everyday unhappiness. Imagery can eradicate the needless pessimism that so often corrodes our self-esteem and that produces apathy, lethargy, and self-criticism.

As discussed in Chapter 1, different images produce different feelings and emotions. The images that give rise to sadness tend to revolve around some type of *loss*. There is a void, an emptiness. (Anxiety, on the other hand, is often the result of images about some *threatened* or impending loss). It cannot be overstated that people's feelings and actions are carried out in accordance with what they *imagine* to be true about themselves and their environment. The late Dr. George Kelley identified one of the most fundamental principles in psychology. "A person's processes are psychologically channelized by the ways in which he or she anticipates events." The most significant word in the preceding postulate is "anticipates." It implies that human beings are governed by their predictions of the future. And, as we have been emphasizing throughout this book, most of our optimistic and pessimistic anticipations take the form of mental imagery. We are often asked, "What do you see yourself doing five years from now?" One of my junior colleagues stated that he saw himself doubling his present income within five years, that he pictured himself completing two basic textbooks, that he visualized himself buying his own home, driving an expensive car, improving his tennis game, and learning to play the guitar. Was he optimistic because he focused on positive imagery; or did he focus on positive imagery because he was so optimistic? It is my strong conviction that the former reason is correct—imagery spawns optimism or pessimism.

To cite a case in point. I was consulted by a middle-aged woman who was recently divorced. She complained of great unhappiness, pessimism, and loneliness. "I can just see myself growing into a pathetic old and unwanted wretch," she said. What an unfortunate image! Anyone with that negative prediction was almost bound to be miserable. I immediately set about trying to help her to alter that gruesome image. We started by listing a variety of things that she used to find interesting, stimulating, or enjoyable. These were ordinary activities, such as taking walks in the woods, visiting museums, attending concerts, playing with her younger sister's children, eating ice-cream, reading magazines, and so forth. As a homework assignment, I asked her to imagine herself carrying out these formerly enjoyable activities. "Just bathe yourself in these enjoyable images," I advised, "and make sure that you do so for at least fifteen minutes twice a day. Let your mind drift and roam around, but as soon as it dwells on a negative image think of a huge STOP sign, and switch onto any pleasant scene."

When I saw her a week later, she had carried out her imagery exercises and was feeling less sombre. Next we started thinking about various realistic possibilities for her future. What positive steps could she take that would alter her pessimism? Her chief fantasy was that some man would fall in love with her and solve all her problems. I called this a "parasitic image" and stressed that it was generally a bad idea to base one's happiness on the essential presence of another individual. My point was that whereas a romantic male-female relationship would be fine in its own right, she needed to acquire a repertoire of happiness-producing stimuli with or without a man in her life.

While discussing her options, it became clear that she lacked a specific goal. After some discussion, she said "I'd love to go into real estate, but I don't know if I have the self-confidence." I asked her to practice systematic imagery with regard to selling real estate. "Picture yourself interviewing clients, see yourself discussing with them the type of home they desire and require, see yourself showing them various houses, visualize it all very vividly. Do this several times a day. And also make enquiries about studying for the real estate license.''

She arrived for her third, and final, session in a spirit of joy and optimism. ''I can see all sorts of possibilities, with many interesting things to do. . . . I have definite plans for my future.'' Once again, a change in imagery had produced a change in feelings. The image of the ''pathetic old wretch'' had been replaced by that of an interesting and interested person pursuing a variety of stimulating activities, deriving pleasure from everyday events, together with the cultivation of various goals and sub-goals in life. She had by no means abandoned the hope of effecting a romantic liaison with a worthwhile man, but this was no longer an essential condition for her continued happiness.

A follow-up inquiry one year later revealed that she had obtained a license to sell real estate and that she had been successful in this endeavor. She had been involved in a few love affairs, but none of her romances had led to a lasting attachment. She had become extremely interested in anthropology and was taking evening courses at a local college ''just for the fun of it.'' She was currently saving money to go on an overseas trip, and she was seriously considering opening up her own real estate business with two other partners.

TIME PROJECTION OR TIME TRIPPING

The truism ''time heals'' is misleading. It is not the passage of time per se that does the healing.

Imagine that Rip Van Winkle had been hurt or upset by something soon before falling into his twenty-year-long sleep. When he awakened, although two decades had passed, he would probably still feel upset by the incidents that had occurred twenty years before. The passage of time ordinarily allows us to engage in *healing responses,* that is to do, feel, think and experience many different things that erase old psychic injuries. Certainly when we think back to relatively minor incidents that may have caused huge upsets ten years ago (or even six months ago!) we often wonder how we managed to over-react so strongly at the time. In retrospect, it simply was not worth the energy, let alone the agony.

When one is unduly upset over an incident in the past, it is often extremely helpful to picture oneself viewing that event retrospectively, from the vantage point of say, six months in the future. For example, one of my friends was excessively upset over just having lost a large sum of money on the stock exchange. "Every time I think of it I go crazy!" he stated. And it appeared that he thought of it a great deal of the time, so much so that his work was suffering, he was hardly eating, and his sleep was filled with nightmares. While he had certainly lost a lot of money, he was by no means destitute, and his reaction seemed extreme under the circumstances. (One might hazard various calculated guesses as to the imagery that was causing his undue upset, but in order to change a negative reaction it is not necessary first to understand it.) I asked him to try out a simple time projection experiment.

"Sit back and relax first. Get into your bodily feelings and let go of any tensions. Just feel comfortably heavy. Feel the force of gravity; a pleasant heavy feeling as you become aware of your own body weight. . . . Now let's imagine that we have a simple 'time machine' that can push you into the future. . . . You first go two weeks into the future. Two weeks have passed. During those two weeks you received your usual salary, plus commissions. . . . Now another two weeks have gone by. You are now one month into the future. During this time you have been receiving your salary plus your commissions. Now let's go further into future time, another five months to be exact, so that you are now looking back to this day from six months ahead. . . . And now let's take a much bigger jump. You are now two years ahead of today, twenty-four months. Think of that vividly. Imagine that two whole years have elapsed. Now look back. What do you see?"

He sat quietly with his eyes closed for about half-a-minute. "Well, for one thing I have kept clear of the damn stock exchange. I have put my money into savings bonds and to hell with the big financial killings." I expressed the opinion that he had learned a good, albeit expensive, lesson. We then chatted about other matters, and by the time he left it seemed evident that he was in a much better frame of mind. When I saw him a few days later, he was back to his old self. "That imagery trip sure did the trick!" he said.

Whenever I upset myself over various issues (such as a dented fender on a new car, an important letter that got lost in the mail, a research grant that was rejected by a university committee, a manuscript that was turned down by a publisher) I always picture myself looking back at the incident from about six months in the future. I instantly realize that a few months from now (or sometimes even a few days from now) it will make very little difference. This produces instant relief. I say "Tough luck!" and go about my business.

Imagery lends itself to various forms of *time tripping*—one can project oneself forward or backward in time. Often, by going back in time and picturing oneself doing things differently, important insights and constructive feelings emerge. Let me cite another personal example. A few months ago I was discussing some formative events and encounters in my professional development with an interviewer. During the interview I said that, in retrospect, I regretted having spent three and a half years in Philadelphia, and that if I had known then what I know now, I would have avoided going there. My sojourn in Philadelphia was unpleasant for many reasons and I had believed that the time I had spent there was a complete waste. Upon hearing my account, one of my colleagues suggested that I should try out some time tripping. I agreed, and under his direction I pretended that the year was 1967 and instead of going to my new position in Philadelphia I elected to go elsewhere.

I rewrote my ticket, by-passed Philadelphia, introduced some pleasant events, remained in California, and then pictured myself toward the middle of 1970 after *not* spending three and a half years in Philadelphia. In the imagery, I saw myself feeling relieved and happy at missing the negative events that had really taken place during the period I had spent in Philadelphia. The time tripping sequence involved a series of events that all added up to having a much better time personally and professionally in California. Using time projection, I then continued my journey from 1970 to 1972, and then in two-year periods until 1978.

As the time projection brought me nearer and nearer to present time, I realized two important things. First, it struck me that without having experienced certain negative things in the past, I would be less able to appreciate certain positive ingredients in the present. (For example, if you have always lived on gourmet cooking, the next gourmet meal would be "just another meal," whereas if you gradually worked your way up from bread and cheese to delicious cuisine, you would learn to appreciate good food and be grateful for it.) Second, I saw that the seeds of some important discoveries and some very special present-day friendships were sown in Philadelphia, and that by eliminating those three and a half years I would be losing some vital links to the present. The immediate and lasting impact of that time tripping exercise was to wipe away my regrets at the so-called wasted years I spent in Philadelphia.

Recently, I applied time tripping to a rather obsessional woman who was driving herself crazy by ruminating over a feeling that she had married the wrong man. Four years ago she married a man whom she had been dating for about nine months. Before that, she had been engaged to a man for over two years, but she broke off the engagement because her parents disapproved of her fiancé, and because he kept postponing their wedding date. Two weeks before marrying her husband, her former fiancé had come to her and asked her to marry him. When she refused he said, "You are making a serious mistake!" Although her marriage was successful and she had a 3-year-old child whom she and her husband loved deeply, she remained haunted by the notion that she had indeed made a terrible mistake, that she had married the wrong man. "I think about it all the time and I don't know what to do!" I suggested that we try some time projection into the past. After relaxing her, I asked her to imagine that she had agreed to marry her former fiancé. I had her describe very vividly her day-by-day existence with this man. I asked her to imagine herself sleeping with him, making love to him, waking up with him, going visiting with him, and so on. I paid particular attention to scenes involving her parents and the impact of their tacit disapproval. She then directed some of the imagery herself. She pictured having his child and what sort of a father he would make. She imagined herself dealing with various household matters, finances, leisure time, and so forth. After the time tripping exercise she said, "I feel miserable—no, *bored* would be a better word—at the prospect of being married to that man." After that single imagery excursion, she was no longer troubled by the nagging thoughts about having made a mistake in her marriage. (Some people may be inclined to point out that she was merely "playing tricks with her mind," that she was eager to convince herself that her marital choice was not ill-founded. This might well be the case, but it ended four years of nagging doubt in a matter of thirty minutes!)

The use of time projection in "mending broken hearts" can be extremely effective, as the next section will show.

BROKEN LOVE AFFAIRS

In my clinical practice, one of the most frequent problems that lends itself most readily to time projection images is broken love affairs. When a loved one finds someone else, or whenever romantic attachments come to an end, much psychic pain usually ensues. Few situations lead people to evaluate themselves as thoroughly as the self-questioning that usually follows a broken love relationship. One questions almost every facet of one's being. Rejected lovers suffer acute pain as a result of probing questions and resultant self-doubts. Am I stupid? Am I unattractive? Am I sexually incompetent? Do most people simply put up with me? Am I really worthy and capable of loving and being loved?

These questions set off a chain reaction. The rejected lover usually perceives the rejector as particularly invaluable. Suddenly he or she becomes invested with only positive qualities. The rejector is a prince or princess, he or she alone in the universe is capable of bringing sustained happiness and meaning to the life of the rejected person. A compulsion sweeps into operation. "I must have him/her back."

To break this compulsion, I employ time projection by asking the sufferer to go forward in time and to picture her or himself engaging in various rewarding activities. For example, I will say: "Let's go forward in time. Picture yourself living through today and tomorrow. Now, you can easily sit and mope, cry and eat your heart out, hope and pray that your beloved will return, and continue to feel desperate and alone. But instead, imagine yourself going into a field and painting.* See that scene as clearly as you can. You are in a green field and you are starting to paint or sketch. As the outline of the scene begins to take shape you feel some satisfaction. . . . You also decide to take up the piano again. So now you picture yourself starting to practice the piano, and you feel some satisfaction as your fingers loosen up."

The more sad and dejected the person, the more scenes one employs during the therapy session. The aim is to hit *something* that the person will perceive as pleasant or potentially pleasant, and satisfying. One young man recently proved to be very difficult to inspire. Whatever suggestions I made merely reduced him to tears. Everything brought home to him the fact that Melanie, his girlfriend, was no longer there to share things with him. Finally, we hit upon an activity (horseback riding) that he enjoyed but

* Before suggesting specific activities the therapist first finds out exactly what has been especially rewarding in the past.

did not associate with Melanie. He was asked to picture himself riding horses, enjoying the mastery, feeling the pleasant breeze as he cantered along. This was fairly helpful, in that he stopped crying and entered into the imagery. Above all, he agreed to go horseback riding the very next day. (Parenthetically, his story had a rapid and happy ending. He met a young woman at the riding school, and soon found her far more appealing than Melanie.)

When one views a broken love relationship from the vantage point of "six months into future time" most people discover that there are "many pebbles on the beach," and that it is rather silly to pine over one "pebble" in an overpopulated world. Clinically, I have observed that as soon as I can get a depressed person to admit that some sort of pleasure may be derived from a particular activity, there is an excellent chance of helping that individual overcome the depressed feelings. And when a person allows him or herself to actually *experience* a little pleasure, prognosis is usually excellent. Time projection techniques seem to achieve these ends by encouraging one to think seriously about pursuing options that can lead to fun, fulfillment, and joy. Many people automatically discount the events that can bring joy into their lives. When they feel "down in the dumps," they forget that many enjoyable and fun-filled events are available for their pleasure. Time projection "forces" them to reconsider these pleasurable stimuli and to stop nursing their misery and gloom.

The time projection technique can be used to

cope with rejections of all kinds. Feelings of rejection, feelings of failure, and other aspects of misery and gloom grow stronger when we dwell on the past, on what we no longer possess, on our dashed hopes, and on what could have been if only we had known the right moves at the right time. Instead, when we go into the future, and when we realize that we play a large role in shaping that future, our mood becomes one of buoyant anticipation. The process is to picture oneself going forward in time, carefully planning a range of positive steps one can take day by day, week by week. It is essentially a self-programming technique. As the negative, self-defeating, dismal images come flooding in, they are deliberately forced out of the mind. Sometimes, one has to scream inwardly to oneself: "STOP! I refuse to think those thoughts!" and then one inserts the positive images over and over again.

Time projection is a method that helps one get through the present when, for whatever reason, the ongoing events are less than pleasurable. Thus, when one of my students contracted rheumatic fever and was bedridden for over three months, I helped him over the crisis with time projection. He was despondent because he would be losing an entire semester, and he had hoped to embark on his dissertation just before becoming ill. Using time projection, we first went forward about six months into the future. He could then look back on his illness, feel pleased that he had taken good care of himself and not rushed back to work prematurely, and by that time, he could be well on his way toward catching up with his work on his dissertation. We then went five years into the future so that he could look back and realize that by then, it would make very little difference to him whether he finished his studies this year, or even two years later. Again, as with most imagery methods, when we take the time to *visualize* events that lie ahead of us, we automatically increase the likelihood of achieving self-fulfilling outcomes. Time projection is a way of permitting "knowledge by description" to become like "knowledge by experience."

IMAGES OF MASTERY

A theory of "learned helplessness" put forward by Dr. Martin Seligman of the University of Pennsylvania can account for certain forms of depression. People who are unassertive, self-conscious, and reticent may, if exposed to insidious and insensitive environments, acquire a firm belief that whatever they try to do is useless so why bother trying to bring about any change? The sequence of events in the development of depression are: (1) first, a high degree of frustration is experienced in attaining goals that the individual very much desires, (2) the person then perceives that his or her efforts make no difference, (3) a sense of helplessness and further frustration confirm this feeling, (4) the belief that one's responses will not receive positive reinforcement then becomes confirmed, (5) the latter results in a reduction in the number of attempts to improve matters, (6) a generalized feeling of helplessness ensues; and (7) depression and melancholia eventually develop.

Dr. Seligman suggests that therapy must show the individual that he or she is largely in control of his or her environment, that the person needs to be taught to achieve mastery and personal effectiveness. I have found that *images of personal mastery* pave the way for various skills that add up to "personal effectiveness." When consulted by a person who seems to fit the learned helplessness model of sadness or depression, I start by finding some little task that the person can perform well but nevertheless avoids doing. I believe that everyone can do something well, be it embroidery, painting by numbers, arranging furniture, fixing faucets, washing cars, chopping wood, adding numbers, remembering songs, or whatever. I relax the person and then ask him or her to picture him or herself doing whatever thing he or she does well. We enter into the scene vividly, and introduce the feeling of mastery that accompanies anything well done.

Many people express a "so what" attitude to these minor personal accomplishments. They argue that fulfillment in life requires a lot more than the ability to fry an egg or polish a brass vase. I quote Benjamin Franklin, who said: "Human felicity is produced not so much by great pieces of good fortune that seldom happen, as by little advantages that occur every day." In imagery, we concentrate on those "little advantages." The person whose short story is published in a local magazine need be no less happy than the nuclear physicist whose mathematical formula is published in a prestigious journal. Of course, it is simple to negate each and every accomplishment by comparing it to the great achievements in human history. The physicist who feels that nothing less than the Nobel Prize warrants personal gratification and joy will almost certainly be a victim of constant frustration, possibly leading to learned helplessness and depression. Abraham Lincoln pointed out that *"Most folks are about as happy as they make up their minds to be."*

A case in which images of personal mastery helped to overcome an intense state of depression may round out this discussion. A 54-year-old woman had suffered a stroke that left her somewhat incapacitated. The left side of her body was weak, and she tended to drag her left leg when walking. Prior to her illness she had been an active golfer and a skier. She not only excelled at these sports and enjoyed them, but she received a good deal of praise and admiration from other people for her skill and agility. Now she was unable to participate in these activities and she became listless, disgruntled, and more and more miserable.

Her husband persuaded her to consult me and came along to the first session. "All the fun has gone out of her life," he said. She was indeed most unhappy and declared that she might as well be dead but lacked the courage to kill herself. I felt that she needed antidepressant medication and asked her to see one of my colleagues, a psychiatrist, who would

143

prescribe the proper medicine. She refused. "Can't we do something other than put me on pills?" she asked.

I decided to see if she would respond to images of mastery. In searching for something apart from golf and skiing that she could perform very well, we finally came up with a rather fancy cake for which she had a special recipe. In imagery, I had her clearly visualizing the details of preparing the cake step by step in anticipation of a dinner party at her home. In the images the culminating experience was the amount of praise and the compliments she received for her excellent meal, and particularly for the special cake. "You can't compare that to winning a golf match!" she protested. I explained to her that she was to avoid making comparisons but that she was to concentrate solely on the pleasure that comes from any task that is well done—in her case, baking a special cake.

There were other things that she did well. She was good at several card games from canasta to poker; in addition to her special cake recipe she was in fact an excellent cook; and she had been a pretty good amateur photographer in her youth. Accordingly, in imagery, I had her dwelling on each of these specific areas in turn, without comparing them to golf and skiing. She was to picture herself exploiting each of her positive attributes one by one—seeing herself learning more about poker, enjoying the thrill of an exciting bid, winning the jackpot. Next, she would clearly imagine herself preparing and serving a gourmet meal. When picturing herself performing each of these activities, I asked her always to get in touch with her own subjective feelings of mastery.

These images of mastery served a dual purpose. First, by concentrating on these positive skills within herself, her own gloomy and depressed feelings started to abate. Secondly, these scenes served as a goal rehearsal (see Chapter 4) so that I was not surprised when she told me that she had once again taken up photography and that she was saving up money to buy some equipment with which to furnish a darkroom in her basement. Here we see another example where depression can escalate when someone dwells on particular losses instead of looking to one's assets and positive outlets. Merely telling somebody not to rekindle self-pity and misery seldom has a positive effect, but when we employ imagery, significant changes often come into being.

The ability to derive full pleasure from a simple task well executed is a skill worth cultivating. Picturing oneself attaining these minor goals in imagery, and then going out and performing the actual tasks, is one of the best antidepressants. It has many other important ramifications, and forms the subject matter of our next chapter.

CHAPTER 9

Imagery for Overcoming Psychosomatic Disorders

Some of the imagery procedures used by certain practitioners are based on spiritual and mystical notions. Religious healers often invoke the image of "walking with Christ" in order to facilitate self-confidence and to achieve other spiritual ends. Some healers believe in "magic fluids" and they encourage their patients to picture themselves applying these special substances. In Europe, many of the physicians who use imagery techniques prefer to track the free-flowing scenes that accompany introspection, instead of generating specific or controlled images under the direction of a therapist. Those who use the latter approach often do so in order to understand the putative symbolism behind the imagery. This is especially true of psychoanalytically oriented clinicians who interpret each image in terms of sexual drives, phallic symbols, birth fantasies, castration fears, displacements, resistances, and so on. Other than anecdotal reports of impressive results, there are no data to demonstrate that imagery used in this manner produces predictable and reliable changes. On the other hand, there are several studies that show precise cause-and-effect sequences upon administering the imagery techniques described in this book.

A CURE FOR STOMACH ULCERS?

Throughout this book, we have avoided fanciful notions. We are concerned only with imagery techniques that have at least a modicum of experimental validity and that possess immediate clinical utility. The literature on psychotherapy is replete with all sorts of anecdotes regarding esoteric methods. Unfortunately, too many people tend to prefer nebulous concepts to clear-cut ideas. But perhaps certain "way out" notions may contain some merit. For example, one of my associates claims that he cured his own stomach ulcer by means of imagery. During the course of six or seven weeks, he spent a period of twenty minutes each day (ten minutes in the morning and ten minutes in the evening) picturing himself taking a journey through his own body. He vividly imagined himself aiding and adjusting his various internal organs. Thus, he would think of himself massaging his kidneys, liver, gall bladder, and spleen, and when he pictured himself entering his own stomach he would go straight to the "ulcer crater" and imagine himself administering various soothing and healing substances. According to him, this imagery technique cured his ulcer in less than two months!

There are much more fantastic reports than the foregoing; some of them are extremely involved and intricate. Whether or not there is actual merit in such procedures is scientifically unknown at this time. Papers presented at the International Society for Mental Imagery Techniques have described impressive results from the varied use of images, which range from the slaying of dragons and dreadful monsters to that of peacefully following a brook to its source. Indeed, many respected practitioners have reported all sorts of positive outcomes from a large variety of imagery procedures. From a scientific standpoint, this is insufficient and does not constitute "data." There are too few controlled experiments and far too little systematic research into these methods.

Yet, while too much reliance cannot be placed on any individual practitioner's reports, it is unwise to dismiss testable claims of therapeutic benefits that can accrue from imagery procedures. The psychosomatic potential of imagery techniques is easily demonstrated. There are many studies showing that people can learn to control heart rate, body temperature, blood pressure, and several other physiological processes. The work on biofeedback, in which special machinery is used to teach people how to monitor and control autonomic nervous activity, has become an important area of clinical research. But one does not necessarily require machinery to achieve these ends. Imagery alone can often be used for these purposes. For example, the famous Russian research psychologist, Professor A. R. Luria, described how one of his subjects was able to alter his pulse rate from 70 beats per minute to 100 beats, and then back down to his normal pulse of 70. The subject said: "I simply saw myself running after a train that had just begun to pull out. I had to catch up with the last car if I was to make it. Is it any wonder then that my heart beat increased? After that, I saw myself lying in bed, perfectly still, trying to fall asleep. . . . I could see myself beginning to drop off . . . my breathing became regular, my heart started to beat more slowly and evenly." Similarly, by imagining himself touching a hot stove with his right hand, he raised the actual skin temperature 2 degrees. At the same time, he lowered the temperature of his left hand by 1½ degrees. He simply pictured himself holding a piece of ice in his left hand. "I could see it there and began to squeeze it. And, of course, my hand got colder." Professor Luria and his colleagues also demonstrated that it is possible to control the size of the pupils of the eyes by means of imagery. One visualizes various degrees of light. For instance, one of their subjects imagined a very bright light shining directly into his eyes, and the pupils of his eyes contracted accordingly. Let us now turn to the use of imagery in overcoming psychosomatic disorders.

HYPERTENSION

I was consulted by a man in his late forties who suffered from high blood pressure. His physician had placed him on medication for his hypertension, but the medicine produced two unfortunate (but by no means uncommon) side effects. He became sexually impotent and developed depressive reactions. Without drugs he was potent and undepressed, but he had headaches, dizziness, and some fainting spells. He was told that transcendental meditation would lower his blood pressure, and he enrolled in a TM class. While the meditation did prove helpful, he found it extremely boring and stopped practicing it after three months.

I suggested the use of *positive imagery* instead of meditation, twice daily for twenty minutes at a time. He described three different scenes that produced feelings of calmness and tranquillity. His first scene was a large meadow with a few cows, a stream, some trees, and fleecy clouds in a blue sky. The second scene was inside a warm sleeping bag in a tent pitched in a valley, alongside a high mountain. The third serene image was of a soft raft, floating in a large swimming pool on a hot Sunday afternoon.

Each morning upon awakening, before breakfast, he was to relax, close his eyes, and visit any one of these scenes for about twenty minutes. If his mind wandered from the scene he was to gently coax it back again to the farm, the tent, or the raft. He was to visit any of these sites once again, for about twenty minutes, before dinner.

The similarity of this imagery method to certain meditation procedures is obvious. However, many people have told me that, whereas they soon found themselves becoming bored with meditation, they were always able to conjure up new relaxing images when one or more of their scenes became boring. Hence they were much more inclined to continue practicing the imagery exercises. The man referred to above has now continued using positive imagery for the past two years. His blood pressure no longer constitutes a problem.

Some people have inordinate difficulty accepting straightforward and simple ideas. For them, unless mental exercises have an elaborate rationale they are useless. They are inclined to garnish various ideologies with quasi-religious teachings, add a touch of pseudo-scientific constructs, and pour it into some variant of Oriental philosophy. In my own view, these mental gymnastics are redundant, and usually add chaos to confusion. Throughout this book I have avoided elaborate theoretical discussions, and I have deliberately excluded many imagery methods that do not have a clear-cut rationale.

DERMATITIS

A 19-year-old college sophomore was said to have "hysterical erythema," according to her doctor. Before class tests, and during other periods of stress, her face and neck would develop an inflammation with weals and eruptions. She would then pick at her skin, often causing secondary infections and some scarring. During her high school years she had not suffered from undue tension, and had no dermatological problems apart from some mild acne from time to time. Her "hysterical erythema" first became evident on entering college. However, a few months before attending college one of her closest friends had died in an accident; this friend used to suffer from "atopic dermatitis," an allergic skin reaction that often produces a blotchy inflammation. I carefully discussed several facets of the past interaction with her friend, and came to the conclusion that my patient suffered from undue guilt. She felt that her friend had been much smarter and talented than she, and that it was wrong for her to be in an academic setting. There was no logic to this feeling, but it was strong and persistent. I decided to try some directed positive imagery. I asked her to imagine herself contacting her dead friend and being told that she, the friend, very much wanted her to complete her studies. She was to picture this specific dialogue several times a day.

She followed my suggestion and reported, after a week, that she and her dead friend had discussed "everything that bothered me." (This type of imagery method is frequently employed by Gestalt therapists, who believe that many of us have "unfinished business" that needs to be completed and fully wrapped up.) She then asked me if I thought that she was over-identifying with her friend due to her irrational guilt, and that she was unconsciously trying to turn into her friend in order to assuage her own anxieties. (The young woman had been taking psychology courses in college!) I replied that this was possible, but since there is no way of testing these assumptions and interpretations, they were largely matters of faith. However, after using the simple imagery dialogue, the "hysterical erythma" cleared up and the young woman graduated from college after two years. She is presently in graduate school, where she is doing very well.

In this case, the basic process appeared to be the alleviation of guilt. Many of us carry around small or large burdens of guilt about various negative acts of omission or commission. Guilt is an utterly useless emotion. If we have wronged someone, let us try to make amends. If we are unable to remedy the situation, let us learn from our errors. Guilt achieves nothing for the person who harbors it, and feelings of guilt do not repair damage, cure, heal, remedy, or rectify matters for anyone.

When troubled by feelings of guilt, it is often helpful to see the situation through the other person's eyes (the one about or toward whom guilt is felt) and to realize that he or she is probably willing to forgive and forget. And if that is not the case, the other person probably has big problems!

ULCERATIVE COLITIS

Akhter Ahsen is a psychologist who has developed a most involved and intricate theoretical superstructure of human personality through the exploration of special images that he calls "eidetics." His system of "eidetic psychotherapy" makes extensive use of imagery and becomes deeply involved with meanings and values. However, in order to use the effective techniques generated by Ahsen (or any other therapist) it is not necessary to understand or agree with the theoretical underpinnings. For instance, Ahsen described how he treated a 28-year-old woman suffering from an acute episode of ulcerative colitis. She was in the hospital, passing fifteen to twenty stools a day of blood, mucus, and water. After two weeks, her vital signs were unstable, and she developed cardiac dysrhythmias. Ahsen gave her a simple visual image which she was to practice and recall repeatedly—she was to visualize herself being hugged and embraced, as a little infant, by her mother. Ahsen reports that within twenty-four hours her vital signs became stable. An additional week of further imagery exercises (ten to fifteen minutes daily) decreased her bowel movements from fifteen to twenty stools to no more than five a day. There were also no further cardiac dysrhythmias.

Very few cases are likely to respond as dramatically, but several people maintain that "deeply comforting images out of the past" tend to produce far-reaching effects on the gastrointestinal tract. These comforting images and pleasant memories calm the gut, reduce acid secretion, and tend to decrease spasms and cramps. Under fluoroscopy, one can clearly see how different images produce immediate changes in gastric motility. Physiological effects are by no means confined to the digestive tract. Hostile or hateful images versus warm and loving images produce measurable concomitants in heart rate, blood pressure, respiration, etc. But as we will outline below, aggressive imagery can be therapeutic if properly employed.

SPASTIC COLON

When I have reason to believe that psychosomatic symptoms are a function of suppressed anger, I deliberately encourage my patients to use *aggressive imagery*. Thus, one inhibited and reticent adolescent boy had a spastic colon that remained unresponsive to a variety of medical treatments. It was evident to me that the youngster would bottle up his anger, especially when confronted by authority figures. He admitted to me that there were several people for whom he felt considerable hostility. I told him to imagine himself in a boxing or wrestling ring, having a bout with his antagonists. In the image, he was to see himself vigorously and aggressively boxing or wrestling. He was told to use these images several times a day. Within a few weeks, fortuitously or otherwise, his spastic colon started troubling him less and less. It was then possible for me to teach him how to stand up for his rights in an open and frank manner. This brought further clinical improvement. When women use aggressive imagery, they usually prefer picturing themselves involved in vigorous verbal rather than physical battles. They tend to imagine themselves "telling someone off," or even yelling and screaming. When women do picture themselves resorting to physical violence, they are apt to see themselves kicking, scratching, biting, or slapping—they seldom visualize themselves punching someone.

I have found that many spastic colon sufferers also derive benefit from relaxation and positive imagery, especially images involving the clear picture of one's stomach and intestines becoming more resilient and less sensitive. This image needs to be practiced five to ten times a day, for three or four minutes at a time. The method is very simple. First relax all your muscles as deeply as you are able to, and then picture your gastrointestinal tract becoming less and less sensitive.

TENSION HEADACHES (AND A DRAMATIC CASE OF LONG-SUPPRESSED RAGE)

Most tension headache sufferers derive benefit from relaxation training and biofeedback procedures. Indeed, if you suffer from tension headaches, you would be well advised to try out the relaxation exercises in the Appendix as an initial step. In some instances, no further treatment will be necessary. However, I have seen a fair number of headache sufferers who failed to benefit from relaxation therapy or biofeedback. In many of these cases, their headaches were *anger related.*

It is often helpful to imagine oneself expressing violent anger. Here, it is most important to draw a clear distinction between fantasy and reality. In fantasy, we can picture ourselves killing a million people, but in the realities of life, one needs to cultivate the ability to discharge anger in positive and adaptive ways. In this connection, there are several excellent books dealing with assertive (as opposed to aggressive) behavior patterns. Often, before making a real-life assertive response, it helps to picture oneself "going overboard" in imagery. After discharging the full anger in imagination, one can then carefully rehearse a response that will facilitate the constructive goals one would want to achieve. However, my suggestion here is simply that many chronic tension headache sufferers often find relief from practicing aggressive imagery. For instance, one woman would vividly imagine herself throwing bricks through plate glass windows and she claimed that this image (plus relaxation afterward) would invariably get rid of her headaches. The case outlined below is rather dramatic, but I think it worth sharing in some detail because of its intrinsic interest.

Pent-up Rage

I was consulted by a 48-year-old woman who had been incapacitated by "splitting and blinding headaches" at least twice a week over the past ten years. Doctors (including neurologists and psychiatrists) had variously attributed her problem to unspecified allergies, vascular pressure, eyestrain, and tension. Others thought that she was a classic migraine headache victim. One consultant claimed that her headaches were little more than an attention-seeking device. She had been on special diets, and her treatments (apart from tranquilizers, pain-

killers, and drugs of various descriptions) had included psychoanalysis, diathermy, massage, relaxation, biofeedback, eye glasses, and hypnosis. Some of
these treatments proved temporarily helpful, but
basically she continued suffering from blinding
headaches, and over the years she had resorted to
stronger and stronger painkilling medicines.

Significant events from her life history were the
following: Her father had deserted the family (her
mother, her older sister, and herself) when she was
ten years old. Five years later the father suddenly
reappeared and wanted to return to the family. The
mother refused, and the father shot and killed her
and then committed suicide. The patient lived with a
maternal aunt for about four years and then married. Her headaches started around the time (a) that
her daughter, an only child, left for college, (b) her
aunt (foster mother) died, and (c) she inherited a
fairly large sum of money from her father's brother.
The full impact of these three events were very complex, but upon exploring her imagery, the following
coherent pattern emerged.

Since age ten, when her father abandoned the
family, she felt anger and rage toward him. (Of
course there were many other feelings, but rage was
predominant.) For various reasons, this remained
suppressed. When the tragic murder and suicide
took place, she was numbed by unspeakable trauma,
outrage, fear, and confusion. Her aunt's loving
home enabled her to divert her energies into constructive channels. A succession of events—school-
work, followed by marriage, followed by mother-

hood—enabled her to concentrate on constructive activities. But when she felt her job of mothering was done, when her aunt died and severed a loving link from a sordid past, and when money from her father's family struck her like a crass act of attempted expiation, the long-suppressed feelings from the past could no longer be disowned. She was overwhelmed by feelings of hatred and rage for the grief her father had caused. And she did not know what to do with these feelings, how to cope with the tension, how to handle the searing rage. (Some theorists would consider it noteworthy that her mother had died from bullet wounds in the head.)

Regardless of the accuracy of the foregoing analysis, her imagery was replete with punitive and wrathful indignation at her father's actions. She was totally unresponsive to all attempts to picture her father as a demented person who deserved pity rather than hatred. Consequently, I helped her construct a series of gruesome retaliations that were perpetrated on the memory of her father. She pictured herself going back in time and torturing him and killing him over and over. She described horrendous attacks that she would imagine launching upon him. In one scene, she went so far back in time that she encountered her father as a young boy—and proceeded to dismember him. I have seldom seen such rage, especially in a person whose demeanor was otherwise most cordial, gentle, sensitive, and kind. When entering her aggressive imagery, she would writhe, sob, snarl, and literally foam at the mouth.

After about three months of (what she termed) "hate sessions" once a week, she reported a distinct improvement in her headaches. Her improvement is still evident five years later.

Few cases are likely to be as dramatic as the foregoing. However, to those tension headache sufferers who do not respond to the usual regimen of relaxation and/or biofeedback, two specific hints might prove helpful. (1) Ventilate your anger in imagery or fantasy. (2) Always remember that in reality anger seldom pays off, but assertive (not aggressive) behaviors tend to yield emotional dividends.

Since the readers of this book will probably fall into two main camps—people who may wish to employ imagery methods to improve the quality of their own lives, and professionals who are interested in adding imagery techniques to their treatment repertoires—I should like to take a few moments to discuss a theoretical point with the practitioners. Upon reading the foregoing case, psychoanalytic therapists will readily identify several psychodynamic principles inherent in the treatment process. Indeed, much of the case would seem to be based on a cathartic model replete with "displacement," "denial," "sublimation," and "identification." It would be a serious error to conclude that I subscribe to these types of explanatory notions or underlying principles. Abreactive procedures can be used without buying into psychodynamic formulations. In other words, one can vividly re-experience strong emotions out of the past without subscribing to

Freudian theories. I have reported the case because it is noteworthy that "rage release" proved effective where so many other procedures had failed. This neither strengthens nor weakens the theoretical underpinnings of any psychotherapeutic system. A strict operant conditioner would have no trouble understanding the positive outcome without recourse to unconscious processes. And let us not overlook the fact that psychoanalysis did not prove successful in her case.

INSOMNIA

People who have difficulty falling asleep often report a marked improvement when using a special kind of positive image. I ask them to think of any place or situation, real or imagined, where they would feel *perfectly safe*. The following are typical: (1) In an indestructible submarine at the bottom of the ocean. (Not for claustrophobics!) (2) In an impregnable spaceship a million light years from earth. (3) In a beautiful, comfortable, but secret room that nobody could possibly find. (4) On a deserted island.

To use the image for soporific purposes, the person gets into bed and takes a voyage to his or her safe place. Thus, one imagines oneself in the submarine at the bottom of the ocean, and all sensations are focused upon the fact that it is completely safe because the submarine is totally incapable of being hurt or destroyed by anyone or anything. (Some theorists will be quick to make interpretations about the presumed meaning behind this type of imagery, but for our purposes these insights are of no value.)

My own favorite anti-insomnia image is that I am attending a most boring lecture which, for unspecified reasons, I have to endure for at least three hours. In the image, we are seated in reclining armchairs and we can lean back comfortably while hearing the speaker's voice droning on and on. In less than three minutes, this image usually induces a deep and restful sleep! Other images that can often induce a deep sleep are (a) imagining work one hates doing, and (b) picturing oneself struggling with boring problems.

IDIOSYNCRATIC IMAGERY

Hypnotists have long claimed that various types of mental imagery can be most valuable for treating a host of psychosomatic disorders. The intriguing connection between imagery and the autonomic nervous system is capable of being researched by the most precise scientific methods. The fact that several present-day experimental psychologists are conducting laboratory research on imagery augers well for the future of this important mode of treatment. Furthermore, now that behavior therapists have shown a growing interest in thoughts, attitudes, images and beliefs (which they call "private events" and "covert processes") we can look forward to excellent clinical research into imagery processes. But from a practical standpoint we do not have to await either clinical or experimental elucidation in order to apply the eminently useful methods outlined in this book.

I would like to reiterate a most important point. There is both clinical and laboratory evidence to show the beneficial effects of protracted positive imagery. In my practice, I make extensive use of "healing imagery" whenever a patient shows signs of stress, tension, and psychosomatic disorders. Bathing oneself in positive imagery seems to have a profound effect on the autonomic nervous system. But in some instances, the usual positive images seem to have no effect. Some people need to employ highly personal or idiosyncratic images. For example, several years ago, I was consulted by a 35-year-old man, who suffered from numerous aches and pains (headaches, backaches, stomach aches, chest pains, and various joint pains). Moreover, he was subject to heart palpitations, shortness of breath, fatigue, crying spells, and fits of depression. He had made the rounds of doctors, hospitals, psychiatrists, psychologists, and even a well-known faith healer. Medical tests were indeterminate; psychiatric evaluations ranged from "neurasthenia" to "incipient schizophrenia." But he continued to suffer.

When this unhappy man consulted me he was at the end of his rope (literally and figuratively, since he had made an abortive attempt to hang himself). None of his previous therapists had employed any imagery techniques with him, and I therefore introduced deep muscle relaxation, followed by the usual positive imagery—he was to picture himself on a warm sunny beach with the breakers gently washing

163

onto the sand. This produced little improvement. Meanwhile, we continued discussing certain mistakes he seemed to be making in his day-to-day activities.

He had been somewhat hypersensitive as far back as he could recall, but most of his problems dated back to the death of his mother, when he was twenty-three years old. He had been extremely attached to her, and he found her unexpected death most traumatic. He had many warm and fond memories of his mother, especially of things they had shared when he was a little boy. "I recall my tenth birthday party very clearly, and I can see the cake, the candles, and all the other kids. . . . I can see my mom smiling at me and this brings back happy memories." I asked him to substitute the tenth birthday image for the beach scene, so that at least twice a day for about ten to twenty minutes, he would relax and relive his favorite birthday party. At the end of one week he reported feeling somewhat less anxious.

As we discussed his feelings in greater detail, he recalled a story that his mother had often told him at bedtime when he was a child. It involved a "window in the heaven" through which one could pass and play with the angels. He associated this fantasy with very profound peace. Accordingly, we agreed to switch the tenth birthday party image he had been practicing to the "heavenly window" image. Again, at least twice a day, for some ten to twenty minutes, he was to bathe himself in this image.

He told me how he would often amplify this

image. As time passed, and as he used the image more and more, he developed special friendships with certain angels who eagerly awaited his twice-daily visits. On occasions, he was privileged to see God in the distance, and he would also spend time with his mother through the heavenly portal. At the end of twenty minutes, he would return to earth. While his treatment consisted of many other modalities—he learned new and more useful behaviors, how to handle his emotions more maturely, how to become more attuned to his sensations, how to dispute false beliefs, and how to deal more openly and effectively with other people—a dramatic improvement in his overall condition followed his twice-daily imagery excursions through the "heavenly window." The aches and pains cleared up; there was no depression, no shortness of breath, no tachycardia. He took a job on the West Coast, and I lost touch with him for almost three years. Recently, I gave a talk in Los Angeles, and he was in the audience. Afterward he came up to me and mentioned that he was doing very well. He was married, and his wife was expecting their first child. He smiled, and remarked somewhat cryptically, "I still pay my visits twice a day."

Some therapists may question the wisdom of employing fantasies with people who are inclined to daydream, or who are somewhat out of touch with reality. I have seldom found someone who could not separate the deliberate use of imagery or fantasy from his or her day-to-day realities. Perhaps this is because I emphasize to my patients that they must always make this critical distinction between the real and the unreal.

One may ask what process or mechanism lies behind the clinical effectiveness of positive imagery. I am of the opinion that the healing factor is the profound degree of relaxation engendered. There are numerous studies that show penetrating physiological and biochemical changes during and after periods of relaxation. Note that the term "relaxation" refers to the deliberate letting go of muscle tension. Many people say "I relax with a good book" or "I find TV relaxing." They are confusing relaxation with recreation. While recreation is both positive and important, *it is not the same as systematically and deliberately sitting down, letting go of your muscular tension in a progressive pattern, so that deeper and deeper levels are attained,* and then dwelling on positive imagery, so as to create still deeper and more satisfying concomitants of the relaxation response. The combined use of relaxation and mental imagery may be likened to hypnosis and self-hypnosis, because altered states of consciousness are produced. But whatever the ultimate explanation may be, there is empirical evidence that attests to the remarkable benefits that can accrue from the regular use of imagery as described in this book.

CHAPTER **10**

Imagery for Preventing Future Shock

What Alvin Toffler aptly termed "future shock" refers to the fact that we often fail to anticipate important future events, or keep up with change. We then become overwhelmed, disoriented, and disorganized. As Paul Valéry wryly remarked, "The trouble with our times is that the future is not what it used to be."

Recently, much has been written about the so-called "male menopause." In this age of increased self-awareness and self-actualization, a "fringe detriment" has been a greater degree of self-consciousness. People seem to find it difficult to grow old gracefully. Popular and professional books now underscore the typical psychosocial stages of adult development—what to expect between the ages of thirty and forty, forty and fifty, fifty and sixty, sixty and seventy, and perhaps even eighty and one hundred. But many individuals seem to be caught by surprise. Instead of easing gently and effortlessly into successive stages of life, they seem to wake up suddenly at age forty or fifty and realize that "middle age" is upon them. Sometimes panic ensues.

I remember seeing a man who was acutely depressed. He was forty-six years of age and although his objective circumstances were enviable—good job, good family life, good money—he plummeted into a melancholic state when he learned that his favorite restaurant was closing down to make way for a supermarket. He came to the uncomfortable realization that "nothing is the same." As he took stock of his life, the closing of the restaurant showed him how many other things had changed, and he was struck by the realization that his youth was gone and that several things were sealed off from him. On a business trip to Chicago he decided to visit his childhood home, only to discover that it had been replaced by a large apartment building. And when his 21-year-old daughter announced that she was about to get married, he was taken completely unawares. He had been so preoccupied with business matters that he was marginally aware of the fact that his daughter was no longer thirteen. Suddenly, from his perspective, his child was a 21-year-old woman.

At the time, I wondered if his depression could have been prevented if he had prepared himself for these inevitable changes. This idea was strengthened by some data I obtained from follow-up inquiries. It appeared that several ex-clients had maintained their recoveries until some significant, but eminently predictable, circumstance took them by surprise. For example, one young woman whom I had successfully treated for extreme anxiety remained free from tension and fear, until her father, who had previously suffered two heart attacks, had a third coronary thrombosis and died. She had a complete relapse and required several months of additional therapy before she was free from anxiety again. I asked myself "What would have happened if, before discharging her from therapy the first time, we had done something more than merely talk about her feelings regarding the fact that her father might soon suffer a fatal heart attack?"

How do you prepare someone to cope with events that may lie in the future? Rehearsal through projected imagery is an obvious strategy. I started looking beyond the past and present problems of my patients or clients, into their most likely *future problems*. Apart from helping them solve their ongoing problems, I carefully examined the probable changes that were likely to occur in their overall life circumstances within the next five to ten years. Thus, the young married couples who were receiving marriage counseling were likely to become parents, with all the attendant problems and responsibilities, if the marriages continued. Many of them, according to present statistics, would see their marriages break apart and would have to adjust to the trauma of divorce. Certain business executives were likely to be promoted and/or moved to new locations.

Others might well be passed over for promotion and have to handle that hurt, or be forced by company policy to retire. Some people would face an empty nest, with children leaving home for college or jobs, or to get married and start families of their own. Others would soon face the death of loved ones, or the illnesses and infirmities that sometimes accompany age.

Many have the philosophy of worrying about or dealing with these events only if and when they have to. "So if we have kids I'll start thinking about it when the time comes." "If the company decides to move us to Chicago, we'll think about it when it's for sure." "My mother is eighty-three. She can't live forever, but I don't like to think about her dying." "I'm not ready to retire. I don't want to think about it yet." Worrying about the future is usually futile; *preparing* oneself for it is quite different. To avoid future shock it is important not only to think about events that are likely to occur in time, it is most important to picture them as clearly as possible, *and to vividly imagine oneself dealing with these situations.*

As Charles Kettering said, "My interest is in the future because I am going to spend the rest of my life there." Of course, everyone knows that it is essential to "prepare for the future," but most people think along these lines in terms of financial security, educational advancement, and retirement plans. Relatively few people actively make plans to acquire the *emotional* equipment to cope with future events.

170

THE GRANDMOTHER

I was seeing a couple whose oldest daughter was engaged to be married. They had made elaborate wedding plans, and were looking forward to having a married daughter and son-in-law. "Have you thought about becoming grandparents?" I asked. Sure, they had *thought* about it. I asked them both to sit back, to relax, to close their eyes, and to concentrate on an image of their daughter being pregnant. We then extended the image to the point where she gave birth, and they were seeing their grandchild for the first time through the glass window in the maternity ward. "Well?" I asked, "how does it feel being grandparents?" The husband opened his eyes, shrugged his shoulders, and said, "Just fine!" His wife, however, looked troubled. "I don't think I'm ready to be a granny!" she exclaimed.

As we discussed matters in more detail, it transpired that the notion of being a grandparent brought her face to face with a range of unsavory aspects concerning age and aging. While exploring other images regarding grandchildren, we found none that reflected anything positive. The picture of telling her friends that she was a grandmother was embarrassing, and images of her own daughter saying "There's grandma!" were most upsetting. The more images we explored the clearer it became that this woman was quite prepared to welcome her son-in-law into the family and to be the mother of a married daughter. But she would have been caught completely unprepared had the daughter become pregnant before we examined and changed her strong negative imagery surrounding the grandparent theme. And it would not have been at all far-fetched to assume that she might have developed a severe depression, or some other "neurotic" pattern, if these themes were left untouched.

In the foregoing case, it became necessary to inject new images and meanings around the concept of grandparent. In place of old age, senility, and other negative associations, we were able to stress the image of being a *young* grandparent. Pictures of people saying "I can't believe you are a grandparent, you look so young!" began to offset the negative elements. The patient was indeed extremely young-looking and attractive. One cannot capitalize on untrue factors. If she were not so well preserved one would require a different line of positive imagery. However, as we embellished the images several other positive themes became evident. For instance, she got in touch with the simple joy of taking her grandchild to the zoo, to parks, and other amusement places, and she developed a feeling of pride and fulfillment and love for a young child descended from her. After a few interviews, she was quite ready to be a wholesome mother, mother-in-law, and also a creative grandmother, if and when the occasion arose.

EMOTIONAL "FIRE DRILLS"

The purpose of a fire drill is to prepare oneself to behave rationally and logically in the face of unexpected flames or a blaze. "If a fire breaks out," says the ship's captain, "we will sound an alarm. Take your life vest, which is under your bunk, and immediately come up on deck." Or parents may instruct their children, "If the house catches on fire, do not try to run through the hall. Keep your bedroom door closed and use the rope ladder in your closet." One may rehearse the procedure to ensure that the correct response is likely to follow. The prearranged plan reduces the likelihood of panic, decreases danger, and equips the person with adaptive behaviors—just in case.

The present chapter is concerned with specific ways and means of being emotionally prepared to deal with metaphorical "fires" that break out and cause damage and destruction when we are taken unawares by upsetting (but often predictable) events. The point of an emotional fire drill is to prevent oneself from being caught off-guard or taken by surprise.

For instance, how can one be ready to cope with something like a job loss? Unfortunately, it is common in our society that a person is fired or laid off from a job. People often say, "If I lose my job I don't know what will happen." I would advise such a person to sit down, relax, close his or her eyes, and imagine being unemployed. Then think of all the options, openings, alternatives, and possibilities that one might pursue. It's a lot healthier when a person says something like: "If I lose my job, I will collect unemployment insurance while looking for another job. I will read the newspapers, reply to want ads. I

173

will go from door to door if necessary, looking for jobs. I will ask around. I will try employment agencies. I will call up my old work associates, acquaintances, contacts, even relatives, and distant relatives. Yes, I will be very busy indeed. But right now, I have a very fine job that I hope to keep."

Most people tend to be extremely closed-minded. Of course nearly everyone views him or herself as fair, open-minded, and responsive to sensible or constructive suggestions. Yet, as we observe the behaviors of most people in stressful situations, they display high levels of rigidity and narrow-minded or one-sided thinking. Take the example of a fashion expert whose job in a large and exclusive Fifth Avenue store was closed out. Was she an open-minded person? She thought so. Was she prepared for an emergency? She would say "certainly." What would she do if she were closed out of her present job? Simple. She would get another job such as hers. Had it occurred to her that she might not be able to obtain such employment? No, not really. But that's what happened. During the recession she found herself among the unemployed. There were no new jobs for such high-paid experts. Now the point is that this woman was extremely talented. If she had given some thought to various ways and means in which her many talents could be put to use, she would soon have found gainful employment. If she had thought through her options, if she had pictured herself in the tough spot of having no job, and if she had visualized herself exploring and finding alternative activities, she would have avoided much grief.

A different type of work-related situation is the make-it-or-bust phenomenon. Another way of putting it is, "I'm either going to be NUMBER ONE or nothing!" Thus, a young ballet dancer had her sights set on becoming the principal or prima ballerina. While she was reputed to be an excellent dancer, her chances of being regarded as truly outstanding in a field as highly competitive as ballet dancing were not very good. As I learned more about her situation it became evident to me that, far from being a prima ballerina, she would be fortunate if hired as a regular member of a good ballet company. How would she cope if, in the near future, she realized that she would not be given the opportunity to perform as a ballerina?

To avert an emotional catastrophe I employed imagery by having her picture various auditions where she would dance superbly, but the judges would by-pass her for someone else. Her initial reaction to these negative images was one of anixety, followed by gloom. "I must get to the top!" she exclaimed. I stressed that anyone who places such demands on him or herself is in emotional trouble. While it would be desirable and extremely rewarding to realize her dreams, the flexibility of having other outlets if her ambitions were not achieved would safeguard her from the devastating effects of being without alternative responses. She was a stubborn young woman, but finally the following image broke through her defenses: "If I cannot dance myself, I can see myself opening up a ballet school where I will train young children as ballerinas." I encouraged her to amplify this image by dwelling in detail on how she would organize the school, whom she would hire to work with her, how she would instruct the children, and what additional training she would receive as a teacher. While she is still endeavoring to become a great ballet dancer in her own right, I am more sanguine that if she fails to meet her own level of aspiration the ballet teaching detour will become a viable alternative.

The obvious reality is that too many people do not think things through with sufficient clarity and factual reality to know what lies ahead. "Will you marry me?" proposes the young man. He has a vague and undifferentiated idea of marital bliss. He and his bride will walk hand in hand. At judicious intervals they will be blessed with a cooing baby. In my premarital counseling sessions, I routinely inject the following sorts of images into the romantic scenario. "Your wife has morning sickness. You can hear her retching her guts out in the bathroom." "Your husband is lying sprawled across the bed snoring like a bear." Depending on the exigencies of each case I include images such as arguing about finances, dealing with in-laws, handling differences in child-raising tactics, liking and disliking different people, disagreeing about politics, and so forth. The purpose of these images is not only to introduce a reality-based set of anticipations, but also to permit couples to acquire a rational way of resolving personal differences. Through the use of imagery, one may take a realistic journey into what probably lies ahead. This can prevent romantic marriages from ending in not so romantic divorces.

EMOTIONAL STOCK-TAKING

The main point of this discussion is that it pays emotional dividends to take stock of one's life situation from time to time. We need to examine our current situation, as well as the present forces that seem to impinge upon the significant others in our lives. Thus, a 55-year-old man in a high executive position, took emotional stock as follows: "Right now, I am the president of my company. Within five years I might start thinking about retiring. Now is a good time to picture exactly how I will occupy my time and my energies upon my retirement. My children are all married, and they are now facing the joys and the ravages of being parents. My wife continues to enjoy her work, her interactions with the children and grandchildren, our mutual friends, her own associates, and our frequent trips abroad. I had better start consulting her about the specific changes that might accrue when I retire. We need to end up with the same, or very similar, images." Of course, people do this sort of thing most of the time, but I am advocating a much more thorough and specific way of making future plans. To think of oneself doing x, y, or z is not as valuable as actually *picturing* the events. The image provides a range of possibilities that may be overlooked when only "thinking" about a situation without deliberately going

177

into relaxation as I have described it and *picturing* it.

Three very important areas that need to be worked through in images or pictures are illness, death of loved ones, and changes of career. For example, shortly after her mother died, one of my patients sent me the following note: "I'm so glad you had me living through Mom's death well in advance. It was painful to do the imagery exercises, but in the long run it saved me a lot of hurt. Of course the funeral upset me, but I know that I can accept it because I was properly prepared."

Her mother had been ill for several years and it was clear that she would not live much longer. Nevertheless, the thought of her mother's death filled her with trepidation. "I can't face the thought of it," she told me, "I'm sure I'll go to pieces." Consequently, I encouraged her to practice images involving her mother's death, the funeral, and the aftermath. She resisted doing so because of the intrinsic fears that these images aroused, but I urged her to face up to them.

In her mind's eye she was finally able to picture her mother's death, to see her relatives and friends, to comfort her younger sister, to lend strength to her father. In imagery, I had her going to the funeral, helping with various arrangements, standing by the open grave, and finally attending the wake. Thus, in her own words, she was "properly prepared" to face the situation when her mother passed away. I subsequently learned that while she mourned the loss and wept during and after the funeral, she did not "go to pieces" and was in fact able to lend comfort to others. To prevent future shock in your own life, you would be well-advised to take the following steps:

1. Take stock of your current environment. What are the prevailing forces at work and at home? Think of each one of your meaningful relatives and friends. What shifts and changes are likely to occur in their ongoing life styles? How are these probable changes likely to affect you?

2. Picture these anticipated changes taking place. For example, let us suppose that you are very attached to a family member or friend who might decide to move to a different part of the country so that close contact will no longer be possible. In your mind's eye, you can see yourself missing that person, but you can also picture yourself developing new attachments and having rewarding interactions with someone else.

3. Think about each close and meaningful relationship one at a time. Examine how the present situation will probably undergo changes in the immediate future, or as far ahead as five or six years from now. Then see yourself coping with these changes. It is important that you zero in on a mental image of yourself being reasonably happy and adjusted despite the advent of certain losses or changes that you would wish to avoid.

4. Focus on the probable changes within yourself that are likely to take place over the next five years. See yourself calmly accepting the inevitable. For example, if you are losing your hair, you might

picture yourself five years from now with very little hair, or perhaps quite bald. In your mind's eye, see yourself saying and genuinely feeling, "So what!" or see yourself deciding to wear a wig if that proves less upsetting.

As we mentioned at the beginning of the book, most of our "thinking" involves mental imagery, but by consciously and deliberately focusing on the associated images, the result is a cognitive map that is much clearer and more accurate. In this way, your future plans can be much more realistic and potentially rewarding. You are not caught unprepared or taken unawares. As the future unfolds and becomes a present reality you find yourself ready for it .You have seen yourself there already, and you have visualized yourself coping and surviving.

PART IV

Some
Additional
Imagery
Exercises

CHAPTER 11

Some Additional Imagery Exercises

In my practice of clinical psychology, I soon became painfully aware of a rather obvious fact. You can tell someone exactly what to do, and precisely what not to do, in various situations. Although the person can understand and agree with everything you have said, very often he or she will nevertheless fail to act on your advice. We also fail to carry out what we know will be in our own best interest. For example, Tom declares that it is futile to argue with his aunt, so the next time she talks politics he is determined to stay out of it. However, despite his firm resolution, he finds himself drawn into a heated debate the very moment he next sees her. Or Sarah will say, "There's no good reason for me to feel so nervous and inept around Ellen and Jim. They may have more money (or a better education) than I, but that doesn't make them superior human beings." Five minutes later, Ellen and Jim enter, and Sarah feels inferior once again.

How could Tom and Sarah make their good resolutions stick? In deciding to avoid arguments with his aunt, Tom would achieve this more readily if he also deliberately and repeatedly pictured her making provocative political statements, while he, instead of entering the arena, visualized himself remaining cool, aloof, and uninterested. Similarly, Sarah might picture herself in Ellen and Jim's company while feeling entirely relaxed, calm, and unthreatened in her mind's eye. This image, if clearly focused upon, is likely to achieve far more than her intellectual resolutions.

This chapter comprises some of the most common problems people bring to me as a practicing psychologist. A specific imagery exercise is recommended to decrease the intensity of each problem.

BECOMING LESS CONCERNED ABOUT RECEIVING DISAPPROVAL FROM OTHERS

Practically everyone who consults me is overconcerned about receiving disapproval from others. They do not know how to deal with it effectively. Some people go out of their way to avoid displeasing others, even people who mean relatively little to them. When important people show any disapproval, they feel extremely distressed and depressed.

An effective antidote is to start by clearly picturing oneself at the receiving end of someone's disapproval. Picture the other person's face, his or her voice, posture, gestures, and statements. In the image, one may elect to ignore the attacker, or to defend oneself, to launch a counterattack, or whatever seems appropriate. The point of the exercise is to grow comfortable with the image, so that the anticipation no longer proves troublesome.

For example, a 19-year-old student complained that his father was difficult to please and that "parental disapproval was usually written all over his face." When this happened the young man generally felt troubled and unnecessarily guilty.

I advised him to practice the following imagery exercise at least twice daily. "First relax, and then vividly picture that 'parental disapproval' on your father's face. Get right close up to that disapproving face, as you would with a zoom lens. Study it carefully. See the disapproval. Keep focusing on that look of total disapproval. Keep that image in mind as clearly as you can for at least two minutes."

After less than a week's practice he found that he no longer felt intimidated by his father's stern and disapproving countenance. He would then confront his father and say, "Do you realize, Dad, that you have that formidable look on your face again? What's bothering you?" Before practicing the imagery he had felt too upset and intimidated to verbalize his feelings; he would simply slink away and the tension would mount. "Now I simply confront my father and clear the air."

The therapeutic basis of this exercise is that it combines the desensitization effect (Chapter 5) with goal rehearsal (Chapter 4). Many effective imagery techniques draw upon these two significant psychological processes.

EXPRESSING HONEST OPINIONS

Closely related to the problem we have just discussed is the problem that many people have in expressing honest and open opinions. They refuse to bare their souls unless they are positive that the listener will respond with gentleness and understanding. Unless there is some guarantee that the recipient of the honest and open opinion will display nothing but empathy and acceptance, they prefer to keep their real feelings hidden. In this way, many personal relationships are characterized by a phoniness that undermines genuine caring, trust, and honest feedback. It generally pays to become more frank and forthright in one's interpersonal relations.

A useful imagery exercise is to picture oneself venturing an honest and open opinion that is not well received. Thus, Arthur was afraid to tell anyone that he was homosexual unless he was certain that the other person was broad-minded, liberal, nonjudgmental, and sympathetic to gay people. I advised him to practice seeing himself put down, ridiculed, scorned, and rejected by a succession of narrow-minded, judgmental, unsympathetic and anti-homosexual critics. As I anticipated, by picturing this image over and over, Arthur acquired a fitting indifference to the views of people who were prejudiced, misinformed, ignorant, or hypercritical. Instead of becoming upset, angry, or defensive, he could simply tune them out.

Another type of honest opinion is when one volunteers a well-intentioned but critical comment about, or to, another person who, instead of showing gratitude becomes hurt and angry. Again, picturing these negative consequences repeatedly tends to diminish the fear of facing interpersonal unpleasantness. The net result is the development of more authentic relationships.

SAYING "NO" TO UNREASONABLE OR UNWANTED REQUESTS

The fact that so many people end up saying "yes" when they want to say "no," and feel guilty on those occasions when they do say "no," has been the subject of two popular books. Again, the failure to refuse to accede to the implicit and explicit demands of other people creates considerable emotional suffering. A straightforward imagery exercise that can overcome this problem is as follows: Concentrate on any unwanted or unreasonable request from a person, to which you generally say "yes" although you want to refuse. You need to think of something actual and specific in your home, or at work, or with a friend, etc. Then picture yourself tactfully but firmly declining. Rehearse this scene several times a day.

As you picture yourself saying "no" (and always imagine yourself doing so firmly but tactfully) you will probably be aware of certain tense feelings. Concentrate on these tensions and see what other images emerge. Then deal with these images one by one using any of the methods you have learned from this book (or elsewhere). Here is an example: Betty's employer had taken her to lunch on two occasions and was making more serious advances. She was not interested in pursuing more than a work relationship, but she was afraid to say "no" for fear she would lose her job. She was earning considerably more than she could hope to be paid elsewhere. As she practiced the imagery exercise she pictured herself saying, "I don't think that we should get involved outside of work." As she imagined the scene she felt tense and somewhat anxious. Upon dwelling on her tense feelings, a clear image arose of her employer saying "You're fired!" This image elicited an assortment of scenes—walking into her office, clearing out her desk, collecting her pay, saying goodbye to her co-workers, looking for another job.

After dwelling on those images for about ten minutes, Betty felt able to deal with her employer quite directly. She concluded that she would prefer to earn less money elsewhere if it meant having less tension at work. Consequently, she submitted her resignation, and told her employer quite frankly that she felt pressured by his advances. He asked her to withdraw her resignation, and he promised to cease making romantic overtures.

TAKING PSYCHOLOGICAL RISKS

A major cause of emotional misery is the dreary rut that so many people endure because they are afraid to take psychological risks. They decide to "play it safe,'' and thereby lose the opportunity of enjoying many aspects of life. The risks referred to here are very individual. The mere act of inviting a friend to dinner is perceived as an enormous risk by some people. Others are afraid to ask for a raise, to express disagreement, to ask for a date, to reveal an intimate feeling.

Avoidance is perhaps the greatest factor in neurotic behavior. Emotionally disturbed people typically avoid facing other people, avoid facing their own feelings, and constantly find themselves uptight. But everybody is inclined to have neurotic avoidances that hamper some facets of their lives. Perhaps you avoid asking for help or assistance; or perhaps you pretend to be a know-it-all and avoid admitting that you don't know something. Maybe you try to avoid doing things unless you excel at them. Some people are greatly embarrassed about receiving praise or compliments, and go out of their way to avoid them. Others try to do everything in their power to avoid making mistakes, so as to appear perfect or infallible.

The problem of avoidance also ties directly into procrastination—another hallmark of neurotic behavior; and everybody knows how many good resolutions and heartfelt promises are broken, regardless of good intentions. Once more, the systematic use of imagery can help to overcome these emotional problems.

The following imagery exercise has helped hundreds of people break their negative habits of avoidance and procrastination:

First, make a list of any unpleasant situations that you have been avoiding. For example, visiting a sick friend; telling your parents to stop interfering with you; studying for an examination; paying back money; writing a letter.

Next, pick any item on the list and vividly picture yourself carrying out the necessary action. Do it again and again for at least three to five minutes at a time.

You are best advised to start imagining those items that are easiest for you. After rehearsing them in imagery, go out and perform them in reality. Then you can gradually and systematically increase the difficulty of the tasks you set for yourself.

As the list of situations you previously avoided grows smaller there will be a progressive gain in self-confidence, self-worth, and personal mastery. You need to realize fully that effort is necessary to bring about constructive change. Deliberate and specific imagery exercises are probably among the most effective ways of ensuring a brighter psychological future.

THE ZERO REACTION IMAGE

Here is another imagery exercise (developed by Dr. Joseph Cautela of Boston College) that many people have found effective in calming their own fears. Let's say that someone is extremely afraid of asking a question in class in case he or she appears foolish. In the image, one is to picture oneself asking a most stupid and ridiculous question, a question that is so dumb that other people would be bound to jeer, laugh, criticize, and condemn any person who could possibly ask such an utterly foolish, irrelevant, idiotic question. But in the image, nobody pays any attention, not a single person reacts, there is zero comeback.

I used this technique with a young man who suffered from a mild stutter. He was terrified of making any public speeches, but he was enrolled in a college course that called for verbal presentations. I had him picture a situation in which he was addressing his class, but in the image his speech was so bad that hardly a word got out without a prolonged speech block. He was to picture the teacher and all his classmates entirely ignoring his extreme blocking. After practicing this "zero reaction" image for a few days, he reported a marked decrease in his anticipatory anxiety. "I don't know why," he said, "but somehow that image helped me lose the fear."

In another case, a woman was afraid to discuss certain feelings with her husband in case he reacted negatively. She used the zero reaction technique. In her mind's eye, she saw herself discussing these feelings with her husband, and in the image, he did not react. She then actually disclosed these feelings to her husband, but in the real-life scene, he did react somewhat negatively. "Instead of feeling terrible, I felt annoyed with him and said that in my eyes he would have earned more respect had he not reacted negatively." Thus, even when the image differs from the real event, the impact of the negative outcome seems to be minimized after practicing the zero reaction image.

CONCLUDING COMMENT

If you have read this book with reasonable thoroughness, and if you have applied some of the imagery methods to your own life situations, I would say that your brain has stored up a great deal of useful knowledge. You will have added significantly to the range of creative solutions within you. If you are fairly inventive, you will be able to devise your own imagery techniques and you will put them to good use. In any event, I hope that you will realize that very little progress will be made from merely reading about imagery. You have to practice imagery exercises *diligently* and *regularly* if you wish to obtain appreciable results. Albert Einstein once commented, "Imagination is more important than knowledge." I hope that this book will enable you to use your imagination in order to acquire greater knowledge, better health, and personal fulfillment.

Appendix

INSTRUCTIONS

Most imagery procedures are more effective if one first achieves a state of general muscle relaxation. Two different relaxation procedures are outlined: (a) alternate tension-relaxation exercises, and (b) sensory relaxation training. Try both types and see which one you prefer. You might ask someone with a pleasant voice to read these instructions into a cassette recorder, or make your own recording. Perhaps you and a good friend can take turns in reading these relaxation exercises to one another. Once you get the hang of it, just do the exercises from memory. You do not have to adhere to an exact sequence.

ALTERNATE TENSION-RELAXATION

Sit down or lie down in a comfortable position. Take in a few deep breaths, in and out, and let your body become loose and pleasantly heavy. Now try to tense every muscle in your body. Tense up every muscle. . . . Now let go of the tension. Let go and switch off all the tension. Notice the feeling of relief. . . . Let's do that again. Tense up every muscle . . . hold the tension . . . relax, let go, ease up, and enjoy the relief. . . . Take in a deep breath now and hold it . . . right in, breathe deeply in . . . and exhale, breathe it all out, and feel the tension going out of the body. . . . Just continue breathing normally, in and out. Each time you exhale, every time you breathe out, feel the tension going out of your body. . . . Now relax the rest of your body, but clench your jaws and close your eyes very tightly. Jaws are tense. Eyes are tight. . . . Keep the rest of the body relaxed, but study the tense feelings in the jaws and in the eyes and face. . . . Relax the jaws and stop tightening up your eyes. Let the jaws and the eyes and the face relax with the rest of your body . . . enjoy the contrast. . . . Now push your head back until you feel tension in your neck. . . . Shrug your shoulders, lift them up. Your neck and shoulders and your upper back should feel tense. Keep the rest of your body relaxed. Study the difference between the tension in your neck and back and the relaxation elsewhere. . . . All right, relax your shoulders, drop them gently down, and let your head return to a comfortable position. Enjoy the sensations and let yourself relax even deeper. . . . As you relax the rest of your body, tighten your fists and also tighten your stomach . . . try to get tension in your hands, your arms, and your stomach. . . . Study that tension. . . . Let go of it. Ease up and allow the tension to disappear. . . . Finally flex your buttocks and thighs, and point your toes downward so that your calves tense up. Feel the tension in your hips, buttocks, thighs, and calf muscles. . . . Keep the rest of the body relaxed. . . . Every part above the hips is relaxed; feel the tension only in and below the hips. . . . And now stop tensing, relax, ease up, and allow the calm sensations to develop and spread. Relax your entire body. As you inhale think the word *"in"* silently to yourself, and as you exhale think the word *"out"* to yourself. Carry on relaxing like this for as long as you like, gently and easily breathing in and out.

SENSORY RELAXATION TRAINING*

Sit down comfortably in a chair so that your back and neck are adequately supported. You will be asked a series of questions. Each question can be answered "yes" or "no" but you do not have to answer the questions in this way. Simply test out your own particular reaction to each question. However you react is fine. There is no right or wrong way.

Is it possible for you to feel pleasantly heavy? (5-second pause)

Is it possible for you to be aware of your hands and arms? (5-second pause)

Is it possible for you to feel that one of your arms is less relaxed than the other? (5-second pause)

Is it possible for you to feel that one of your legs is more relaxed than the other? (5-second pause)

Is it possible for you to allow your eyes to close? (5-second pause)

Is it possible for you to keep your eyes closed

* Adapted from the work of Drs. Bernard Weitzman, Marvin Goldfried and Gerald Davison.

during the remainder of these questions? (5-second pause)

Is it possible for you to imagine the distance from the top of your head to the point of your chin? (5-second pause)

Is it possible for you to imagine that you are looking at something that is far away? (5-second pause)

Is it possible for you to feel the tension going away? (5-second pause)

Is it possible for you to be aware of the space within your mouth? (5-second pause)

Is it possible for you to picture a really peaceful scene? (10-second pause)

Is it possible for you to feel a warm sensation somewhere in your body? (5-second pause)

Is it possible for you to have a calm and secure feeling? (10-second pause)

Is it possible for you to allow your eyes to open? (5-second pause)

If your eyes are not yet open, please open them now and allow yourself to feel awake and comfortable. How relaxed do you feel?

INDEX

Abramovitz, Arnold, 96
acrophobia, 75, 79, 91–92
aging. *See* "Future shock"
agoraphobia, 76
Ahsen, Akter, 153–54
airplane phobias, 5–8, 87–89
alcoholism and heavy drink-
    ing, 113–15
anger, 4
    as cause of headaches,
    156–60
    suppressed, 155, 156
anxiety, 4
    case history, 12–17
    in school problems, 23–24
    techniques for overcom-
    ing, 54–57
associated imagery:
    case history, 12–17
    exercise, 18
    use of, 17–19

Bandura, Albert, 54
Beck, Aaron T., 35, 40
biofeedback, 148–49, 156

brain:
    compared to computer, 41
    images produced by stim-
    ulation of, 42
    left-hemisphere functions,
    43–44
    right-hemisphere func-
    tions, 43–44
    storage function of, 41–42
    synchrony exercises, 44–
    46
    See also Unconscious mind
bridge and tunnel phobias,
    39–41
business. *See* Work and
    work problems

case histories:
    acrophobia, 91–92
    aging, 171–72
    airplane phobia, 5–8, 87–
    89
    anxiety and depression,
    12–17, 129–31, 132–33,
    135–37

case histories : (*cont.*)
   bridge and tunnel phobia,
      39–41
   claustrophobia, 87–89, 92–
      93
   compulsive work behavior,
      111–13
   dark, fear of, 106–8
   dating after divorce, 25–
      26
   dog phobias, 97–99
   personnel problems, 61–65
   psychosomatic disorders,
      147–48, 150, 151–53,
      154
   school examinations, 23–
      24
   school phobia, 99–103
   sexual fetishism, 117–20
   suicide attempts, 120–22
   work promotions, 20–22
Cautela, Joseph R., 91, 114,
   190
children :
   fears and phobias in, 95–
      108
   imagery therapy for, 96–
      108
   motion picture impact on,
      53–54
   negative imagery in, 122
   parents' loss of temper
      with, 55–56

   television impact on, 53,
      95
   See also Case histories;
      Emotive imagery
claustrophobia, 76, 77, 79,
   88–89, 92–93
compulsive work behavior,
   111–13
coping imagery, 89–91, 93

dark, fear of, 95, 106–8
Davison, Gerald, 73–74
dating after divorce, 25–26
death, feelings about, 15–17,
   178–79
   suicide attempts, 120–22
dermatitis, 151–53
depression, 4, 127–45
   case histories, 129–31,
      132–33, 135–37, 143–45
   causes of, 128
   defined, 128
   imagery producing, 128
   "learned helplessness"
      theory, 141–42
   mastery as technique in
      overcoming, 142–45
dieting, 4, 28–29, 115–17,
   125–26
divorce. *See* Marital problems
dog phobias, 33–34, 54,
   97–99

eidetic imagery, 47
"eidetic psychotherapy,"
153–54
Einstein, Albert, 192
Ellis, Albert, 35
emotive imagery, 97–108
advantages of, 97
case histories, 97–103
coping imagery, 104–5
defined, 97
preventive implications
of, 103–5
procedure in, 105–6
Epictetus, 34–35
Evert, Chris, 68
exaggerated role taking, 32,
54–57, 71–72
exercises:
associated imagery, 18
brain synchrony, 44–46
imagery, 38–39, 183–88,
190–92
imagery vividness, 9–11
ISI (Idealized Self-
Image), 27–28
relaxation, 193–96

fantasies. *See* Images and
Imagery
fear(s), 4, 41, 74
imagery therapy to over-
come, 87–94
See also specific fears

Fensterheim, Herbert, 85
Franklin, Benjamin, 142
Freud, Sigmund, 18–19
"future shock," 74
prevention, through im-
agery, 167–80

goal rehearsal, 32, 49, 60–74,
145
in athletic performance,
66–69
for employees, 61–65
for marital problems, 65–
66
for sexual dysfunctions,
73–74
guilt feelings, 152–53

headaches, 156–60
hospital and doctor phobias,
78, 105
hypertension, 150
hypnosis, 8, 71, 113, 166

Idealized Self-Image (ISI),
27–29
images and imagery, 4–5
advantages of, 3
aggressive, 155–56, 157
aversive, 73, 74
and biofeedback, 148–49
and brain stimulation, 42

images and imagery (*cont.*)
clarity level needed for success in, 47–48
as diagnostic technique, 21–22, 23
eidetic, 47
idiosyncratic, 162–65
individual differences in, 5, 30–31, 47
of mastery, 142–45
and meditation techniques, 150–51
in mental training, 48–49
preventive function of, 96
prisoners' use of, 4
as producer of emotion, 27, 128–29
in psychiatry and psychotherapy, 46–47
role in stimulus-response theory, 33–36
as self-fulfilling prophecy, 27, 29, 39, 70–71
storage of, 41–44
underplayed by psychiatrists, 39
unspoken, 31
vividness, exercises in, 9–11
See also Associated imagery; Emotive imagery; Exercises; Imagery therapy; ISI; Negative imagery

imagery therapy, 3–4
for adult fears, 87–94
for children's fears, 95–108
coping imagery, 89–91, 93
homework assignments in, 12
imaginary negative reinforcement, 91–93
self-managed, 11–12
Step-Up technique in, 21–26, 86–87
therapist's role in, 11–12, 17, 165–66
time projection (time tripping), 131–41
variety of techniques in, 87
See also Case histories; Imagery; Negative imagery; specific problems
imaginary negative reinforcement, 91–93
imitation, as therapeutic technique, 54–56
inferiority feelings, 4, 57
in-law problems, 123–25
insomnia, 161–62
ISI (Idealized Self-Image), 27–29
case history, 27–28
exercise, 27–28

James, William, 18–19
Jung, C. G., 46–47

Kelley, George, 128–29
Kettering, Charles, 170

Lincoln, Abraham, 143
Lorayne, Harry, 48
love affairs, broken, 137–41
Luria, A. R., 149

Mahoney, Michael, 69
marital problems, 169,
    176–77
  dating after divorce,
    25–26
  goal rehearsals for, 65–66
  in-laws, 122–25
  misunderstandings, 31
meditation techniques, 150–
    51
memory and mental train-
    ing, 48–49
mental flooding, 86–87
Mischel, Walter, 122
motion pictures, impact on
    children, 53–54

negative imagery, 111–26
  for compulsive work be-
    havior, 111–13

for drinking, 113–15
for overeating, 115–17,
    125–26
and positive rewards,
    122–25
procedure, 111–13
for sexual deviations, 114,
    117–20
for smoking, 114, 115
negativism, 24n, 70
  See also Depression

obesity. *See* Overeating and
    overweight
overeating and overweight,
    4, 28–29, 115–17,
    125–26

Penfield, Wilder, 42
pessimism, 24n, 70
  See also Depression
phobias, 74
  acquisition of, 76
  of adults, 75–94
  causes of, 76, 95
  of children, 94–108
  defined, 75–76
  secondary gains from, 77
  social, 79–87
  techniques for overcom-
    ing, 77–79
  See also specific phobias

powerlessness, feelings of, 12

psychiatry and psycho- therapy, traditional, 8, 71
  human behavior inter- preted by, 37–38, 39, 160–61
  imagery used in, 46–47
  overintellectualization in, 17
  symbolism in, 37–38
  verbal roadblocks in, 17

psychosomatic disorders, 74, 146–66
  case histories, 147–48, 150, 151–53, 154, 155–56, 157–60
  as repressed anger, 155
  See also individual listings

psychotherapy. *See* Psychia- try and psychotherapy

public speaking, 24, 85–86, 191

rejection, 89–90
  and time projection tech- nique, 139–40

relaxation, 193–196

remarriage. *See* Marital problems

role taking. *See* Exagger- ated role taking

school problems:
  examinations, 23–24
  phobias in children, 99– 103

scripts, value of, 64, 65–66

self-desensitization, 82–84, 93

Seligman, Martin, 141–42

sexual dysfunctions, 73–74
  fetishism, 117–20

Shorr, Joseph, 5

shyness, 70, 79

Singer, Dr. Jerome L., 4

smoking, 4, 114, 115

snake phobias, 54

spastic colon, 155–56

sports, 4, 9
  coping imagery for, 91
  goal rehearsal in, 66–69

stage fright, 71–72

Step-Up technique:
  applications of, 24
  for anxiety, 23–25
  for building confidence, 25–27
  as diagnostic technique, 23
  mental flooding in, 86–87
  for school problems, 23–24
  for work problems, 20–22

stimulus-response (S-R) theory, 32–36
  imagery role in, 33–36

stomach ulcers, 147–48
suicide attempts, 120–22
Suinn, Richard, 68
Susskind, Dorothy, 27, 29
systematic desensitization,
77–79, 93
case histories, 80–84
self-desensitization, 82–
84, 93

television, impact on children, 53
tension, techniques in overcoming, 54–57
time projection (time tripping), 131–41
Toffler, Alvin, 167

ulcerative colitis, 154
ulcers, 147–48
unconscious mind, 37–38
See also Brain

Valéry, Paul, 167

Wallechinsky, David; Wal-
lace, Irving and Wal-
lace, Amy, *Book of
Lists, The,* 85

willpower, 115–16, 125
Wolpe, Joseph, 77
women and women's prob-
lems:
aggressive imagery, 155–
56
assertive behavior, 57–58,
63–65
lack of role models in
business, 31–32, 57–58
work promotions, 20–22
See also Marital prob-
lems; Work and work
problems
work and work problems,
57–65
career alternatives, 175–
76
compulsive behavior, 111–
13
goal rehearsal in, 61–65
job interviews, 58–59, 61
job loss, 173–74
of managerial and execu-
tive women, 31–32, 57–
58
promotions and raises,
20–22, 169–70
retirement, 170, 177–78
routine chores, 59–60
sales problems, 60–61
of women, 20–22, 31–32,
57–58